THE FRIENDSHIP BOOK

THE FRIENDSHIP BOOK

The Art of Making and Keeping Friends

Rita Robinson

NEWCASTLE PUBLISHING CO., INC.
North Hollywood, California
1992

Copyright © 1992 by Rita Robinson
All Rights Reserved.
ISBN 0-87877-173-5

Edited by Lorena Fletcher Farrell and Karen Reyes
Cover Design by Michele Lanci-Altomare

First Edition April 1992

A Newcastle Book
First Printing April 1992
9 8 7 6 5 4 3 2 1
Printed in the United States of America

With love to my children, their mates and my grandchildren:

Dawson Busby
Terry (Anhorn) Busby
Julie (Busby) Rogers
George Rogers
Jenny Busby
Jacob Soto
Joshua Soto
Steven Busby
Jeffrey Busby

CONTENTS

ACKNOWLEDGMENTS

My thanks to the countless individuals who contributed to this book.

Gail Kawanami Allen, Ed Asner, Lew Ayres, Creighton Barnes, Joseph Becker, Barbara Booth, Ed Bradley, Anita Baker Bridgeforth, Carole Bryan, Dana Brookins, Danile Brookins, Carlfred Broderick, Fred B. Bryant, Bill Carney, Dame Barbara Cartland, Gordon Clanton, Elizabeth Corson, Barbara Cunningham, Kingsley Davis, Phyllis Diller, Tina Ellenbogen, Ruth Dever, John Edwards, Leslie Elliott, Albert Ellis, Gary Emery, Paula Emick, Lorena Fletcher Farrell, Mark Feldman, Richard Fitzgibbons, Tom Frank, Lawrence Frey, David W. Fulker, Larry French, Shirley Glass, Morley Glicken, Laurence Grimm, Sharlya Gold, Dennis Harris, Shirley Harrison, Leah Hernandez, Thomas B. Holman, Lucile Irving, Alice Isen, Gerald P. Jones, Aaron Katcher, Irwin Jay Knops, Julian Kopit, Paul Kupchok, Rebecca Kuzins, Jack LaLanne, Karl Landis, Lois Langland, Marion Lapins, Mark Leary, Jerry Lee, Paul Lee, Marshall Lewis, Nick and Ellen Livingston, John Lynch, Sally L. Mattson, Ed McMahon, Sally L., Milton Miller, Don Newman, Nell Noddings, Karen Olden, Cesar Romero, Tim O'Sullivan, Lewis Picher, Eric L. Robinson, Bette Ross, Elisabeth Kubler-Ross, Robert L. Rubenstein, Stormy Sandquist, Martin Barry Schlosser, Carol O. Simonton Jr., Dorothy Spivey, Mary Swaney, Phyllis Talasco, Richard Teeling, Irene M. Thorelli, Howard Tinsley, Debra Umberson, Ione Vargus, Dennis Weaver, Ruth B. Weg, Matt Weinstein, Milton Wolpin, Pat Wolff, Phillip Zimbardo, John Zonka.

FOREWORD

Among self-help books, one of the most neglected yet vitally important topics is that of friendship. The self-improvement shelves are bursting with books about marriage, sex, romantic relationships and dealings between parents and children of all ages. (I know, I've written some of them.) But there is very little written about friendship, despite its being one of the most rewarding, enlivening, comforting and loneliness-dispelling human connections we can know.

In my work with people caught in self-destructive love addictions, there is no question that those who are most likely to break free are those who can count on the support, warmth and perspective of caring companions. Friends can also help them deal with the feelings of loss and painful withdrawal symptoms that often follow such breaks, and can keep them from becoming so lonely that they go back to a destructive relationship.

Rita Robinson, a keen observer of human issues, turns her focus in *The Friendship Book* to the importance, value, problems and glory of friendships. This book itself can be a good friend or make an appropriate gift for a good or very dear friend.

Howard Halpern, Ph.D.
Author, *How to Break Your Addiction to a Person*

1 A BANQUET OF FRIENDSHIPS

... those who contribute enjoy the feast

One's friends are that part of the human race with which one can be human.
George Santayana, Spanish-American poet and philosopher

Pat snuggled down in the bed, clutching the tear-dampened pillow. Her sobs were nearly inaudible, but were almost deafening to the two women standing in the room. One of them, a friend of several years, slipped off her shoes and crawled, clothed, into bed with Pat. She wrapped her arms around the grieving woman whose husband had died three days earlier, and held her tightly.

The embrace needed no words, so none were spoken. After about 15 minutes of shared warmth Pat stopped her sobbing, uttered, "I miss him so," rose from the bed and left the room to put on some coffee.

We three sat at the sunlit kitchen table sipping our coffee in silence. Finally, Pat said, "Thank you. I'll be okay now."

Pat knew, as we did, that she would experience terrible loneliness and sadness for months, maybe years, to come, but all would be softened by the embrace of friendship.

Friendship is there in grief and in joy, and it can belong to anyone. Friendship needs no words. It can be present in a room, a gathering, a town, a nation, across the miles. Friendship can mean being there, writing a letter or making a telephone call. It can be wispy, ephemeral, solid or pragmatic, last a lifetime or a week. It can leave

1

with bitterness or stay in the memory like a warm, bright gem. Nothing replaces friendship; not money, power, beauty, possessions or fame.

Dr. Elisabeth Kübler-Ross, pioneer in the movement to humanize the death and dying process, once said to me, "The only thing we'll be remembered for when we die is the love we leave behind."

Friendship is love. And like love, in its broad definition unencumbered by the pettiness of puppy love or the demands of sexual love, it asks that you nurture and respect it, whether fleeting or lasting—for friendship can be either.

Jacques Derrida, controversial philosopher who lectures on friendship, has taught at Yale and is presently at the University of California at Irvine, considers friendship one of the foundations of civilization. Yet he argues with the theme, "Oh my friends, there is no friend." Jewish, he acknowledges that in his early years in Algeria his friends deserted him when Nazism took over.

Perhaps because of his early experiences, Derrida ponders the meaning of friendship more deeply than most.

We take friendship for granted. We may have felt betrayed at one time or another, but we don't like to think too much about it.

Sometimes, however, we're forced to reevaluate friendships.

I recently did some soul-searching when I spent my first winter in a Southern California mountain community that had a 97-inch snowfall in one month. Moving there took me from a mild-climate neighborhood where I'd lived for 12 years. I live alone and work from a home office. A March snowfall triggered landslides on the main roads in and out of the community, which made travel impossible. Busy since the move, I hadn't taken time to get out and about and make new friends. This is a resort town, mostly populated by weekenders. I discovered what it means to have cabin fever. It is a feeling of isolation and loneliness you think will never end. It is when you hear that still, silent voice within, and want it to go away. Had it not been for the phone—which served as a lifeline to my friends and family down the hill—I would have gone completely bonkers. Some friends, and my grown children, believe I came pretty close.

With the arrival of spring I was like the wild flowers that began popping up all over the place. Determined never to be that isolated and lonely again, I made a concerted effort to meet people by attending community functions, inviting people over to dinner, talking to clerks at the little tourist shops that dot the area, and getting to know what few neighbors I have. I also joined a computer group.

Making friends involves risk and chance. I didn't like everyone I met, and I'm certain not all liked me.

Even when a mutually responsive chord seemed to sound, I didn't expect instant friendship. We can never know another person completely, so why should we expect instant friendship? We struggle to know ourselves. We give ourselves space, rationalize our own unacceptable words and actions. Shouldn't we do the same for friends—cherish their differences and idiosyncrasies?

THE GIVE AND TAKE

The maxim that "To have a friend you must be a friend" is true most of the time. Friends don't just tumble from the sky and land in our laps loudly proclaiming, "Here I am. A friend. And I'm perfect to boot."

Some people wish it were that way. They don't realize friendship takes nurturing, care, understanding and time. The husband of a Unitarian minister recounted the story of a woman in his wife's church who moans and groans about her lack of friends. A widow of many years, she says no one ever invites her anyplace. "Truth is, she never invites anyone over to her house for dinner or a party. She sits alone Christmas day because she's too lazy to prepare a feast herself and share it with others. She looks out, instead of in.''

Perhaps she feels that since she's no longer part of a couple, friends are more difficult to come by. Or that because she's no longer young, it's too late to make new friends. Maybe she *is* just lazy. We all have that potential. In truth, the growing population of singles makes the need for friendships all the more pressing, and age need not—*should* not—be a barrier.

When Danile Brookins broke up with her longtime mate, she acknowledges that she had few friends to turn to. ''I realized I didn't have a support system/network beyond my family. I had some friends but they were mostly couples.'' She had allowed her relationship with one person to be all-engrossing. After evaluating her situation, she made an effort to join groups and attend social events. ''I forced myself into situations in which I had no interest because basically I am pretty shy. But I realized friendships don't just come to you.'' So she took chances. ''Finding friends is worth the effort, risk and sometimes rejection,'' she says.

Danile found herself in the same position as many of us. Following my divorce at the age of 40, I was in that spot. My friends had been ''our'' friends. Couples. It shocked and hurt me when even those I had considered best friends disappeared after the marriage ended.

It taught me an important lesson. Don't tie yourself up with expectations; don't sever relationships with personal friends just because your mate is the most important person in your life—and even though he or she might not like some of the people involved. They're your friends, and they are important to your well-being. Because I place such a high value on friendships, when I'm involved in a relationship with a man and he questions any of my friendships, it makes me question my relationship with him.

Both men and women have told me that when some of their close friends become involved with someone of the opposite sex, the friendship wanes until that relationship ends. Then he or she is back, knocking at the door expecting everything to be as it was before. But it's vital to maintain outside friendships during marriage, a live-in situation or even a deeply committed relationship. Not to do so builds resentment, and eventually a good friendship is in jeopardy.

But both men and women need same-sex as well as opposite-sex friends. When I am with my women friends the talk is different than with my men friends, although the topics may be the same. Women have a built-in shared experience. Without explanation, each understands what the other is talking about, and what it means. We connect with emotional nourishment.

Men do too, the well-publicized myth that they don't notwithstanding. It isn't the same type of bonding women share, but that doesn't prevent same-sex friendships from being just as important to a man's well-being as to a woman's.

Expecting a man or woman we're living with to fulfill all our needs is asking a bit much. Deborah Tannen, Ph.D., writing in the bestselling *You Just Don't Understand* (Ballantine, 1990), clearly makes the point that men and women speak a different language.

Most people today accept the *equality* of the sexes; it might be just as important to recognize and accept the *differences* between them—especially when it comes to friendships. Many of us have non-romantic opposite-sex friendships, and we cherish them. I can discuss nearly anything with the few men I count as close friends. I love hearing the male perspective from them.

Yet it's not the same as talking to a close friend of the same sex. The instant understanding, the recognition of shared experiences such as childbirth or thunder-thighs just isn't there when I talk about those issues with men.

Not that women can't or don't talk about the stock market, world hunger, recent wars and sports with the same fervor as men; their talk just sometimes has a different flavor. Men, by the same token, need the familiarity of other men's delivery—it means instant communication without explanation.

We all need spates of intimate, nonproductive, even silly talk. Sharing small, everyday occurrences keeps us human and informed just as readily as do intellectual discussions about world affairs. Unfortunately, we too often lack the opportunity to share these little experiences. Our technological society doesn't provide a ready setting for the spontaneous talk that leads to emotional nurturing and caring.

Consider the time when women gathered along a river's edge to do the family wash. We get an idea of what goes on—women chattering and laughing—when we see films depicting women in India washing clothes along the banks of the Ganges.

How many of you have had a lively discussion with perfect strangers in a laundromat? My first contact with someone from my new community was at the laundromat. We became friends; through her I've met dozens of other people, and she has met my friends. Thus both of our circles have grown larger.

We also witness women milling about and chatting at the open markets of Saudi Arabia. Do you suppose they're talking only about the size of melons?

Primitive men gathered to talk about the hunt. Could they have shared that experience in the same way with the women who were waiting to prepare the meal?

Abraham Lincoln was considered a man's man. He loved storytelling, and early on was the center of attention at male gatherings. We can picture him sitting around the pot-bellied stove of a country store. I'm sure some of his stories weren't considered fit for the ears of the women of that time.

There are still men's men, of course. I have a friend who collects replicas of 19th and early 20th century guns. When he starts discussing them, I fight with myself to pay attention. I'm not good at pretending interest, and he soon changes the subject. He too is a storyteller, and I can picture him telling some of his male friends about his latest gun find, and his joy at catching their interest.

I'm not suggesting that all men talk about are guns and cars and sports—things many women aren't interested in. But whatever the topic of discussion, there are times when it's more comfortable to be with those of the same sex.

When I asked my brother-in-law about best friends, he replied that his wife, my sister, to whom he's been married for more than 30 years, is his best friend. Still, when I had dinner with them and a couple who are long-time friends of theirs, his camaraderie with the other husband was very different from what he has with my sister.

Women have traditionally explored their femaleness and their friendships with other women. Men are just beginning to examine their maleness and friendships with other men. Two recent best-sellers, *Iron John: A Book About Men* by Robert Bly and *Fire in the Belly: On Being a Man* by Sam Keen, show this change. Several magazines, both general and men's, are focusing on the men's movement and masculinity, and a few television sitcoms plan to do the same.

The constraints society has placed on men—admonitions that hugging, crying, and expressed love for another man are unacceptable behavior—often are absent during wartime; men I've questioned about same-sex friendship talk about close, warm, nurturing wartime experiences. This response is especially evident among men who served during the Vietnam era, and we witness it when we see men weeping as they touch the names of lost comrades inscribed on the Vietnam War Memorial in Washington, D.C.

THE COMMUNITY

There is the shared experience between men and women involved in other types of survival. Joanna L. Stratton writes in *Pioneer Women: Voices From the Kansas Frontier*: "To the hard-working family of the frontier, social visits brought a treasured time of relaxation and companionship. While the adults chatted together, comparing notes on crops or livestock or sharing confidences, the children would scamper off to play in the barnyard or explore the nearby creek bed. In the late afternoon, everyone would sit down to supper, and afterward there might be group reading, singing or storytelling by the fireside."

Where do we find this type of friendship—this nurturing—today? It is no less important. Medical research shows our lives may depend on it, just as our forebears counted on neighbors in small communities for survival in an untamed land.

There is more structure in our lives now. The assortment of people we knew who once surrounded us throughout the day have turned into strangers. Those we do know have been compartmentalized. We have friends at work, others at church, others in the organizations we join. There are neighbors, school friends and business acquaintances. We know them, but don't really *know* them, nor they us. We go about our busy day, often oblivious to the needs of friendships. We feel an emptiness even if we're married, and some of us seek the help of a therapist, or even someone such as a tarot card or palm reader. That person becomes our instant friend, and we share confidences as we might have along the banks of the Ganges or in a bombed-out Vietnamese village.

California metaphysician Leslie Elliott recalls a story told him by a client: "When an American lady was touring Greece, she happened to mention to a Greek she met that back home she was the patient of a psychiatrist. To which the Greek exclaimed, 'Psychiatrist? We don't have any here. We have friends.'"

Psychotherapists say that in the last decade people have turned to them for self-disclosure. They come, not necessarily to solve emotional problems, but to have a confidant with whom to share intimacies. This type of sharing used to be with friends from a variety of age groups.

I'm 54 and have friends in their 20s, 30s, 40s—and one of my best friends is 80 years old. I met her in a writing class more than 20 years ago. There have been times when we haven't seen one another for months at a time. Yet when we do get together, it's as if no time at all has elapsed since the last meeting. We share experiences. I can talk to her of my failures and fears. Ruth grew up in New England and has the staunch backbone of people who live in the grips of lashing cold winters. She is one of the few individuals who is free to lecture to me. I don't ignore what she knows about fear and how it can destroy. I listen because we are good friends and she has that right. Our age difference is no barrier; in fact it's an enhancement. Ruth taught me yoga, which she learned at about age 50. She was crippled with arthritis at the time, and it gave her new life. There are no traces of the disease now.

She has served as a type of mentor to me. Now that I'm in my 50s I find myself mentor to younger women, and this is as it should be. While completing a book on Native American spiritualism, I interviewed a tribal woman and learned that the older women—grandmothers, aunts, friends—still instruct the young girls about becoming a woman. This type of instruction is a form of mentoring friendship.

Another friend, when she had just turned 60, quipped to me that she's not making any more friends who are older than she. "Only younger ones. I want someone who can attend my funeral."

My friend's comment may seem cynical, but it emphasizes the need for friends throughout life. There is purpose in friendship, and a need for friends of all sorts. Sometimes we tend to limit friendships to people of like interests and views, which limits our own perspective. On the other hand, a shared interest can open many doors. An interview I had with Miroslav Holub, a Czechoslovakian immunologist and one of Europe's finest poets, illustrates a shared interest in the broadest sense, and although my question wasn't about friendship, it led indirectly to the issue of sharing with friends. Because this was before Czechoslovakia left the Soviet bloc, I asked Holub if he felt constrained in a country that censored the written word.

"It's a trade-off," he said. "Americans, when they get off work, head for the television sets or the bars. Czechs meet with friends for lengthy intellectual discussions, dabble in art, write poetry and make things with their hands—all with feelings of pride."

Because Czechoslovakia is a small nation, even beginning artists and writers receive careful scrutiny and attention from the populace, he said. The country's newspapers review all new writers. "Everyone reads the newspapers and then he or she talks and discusses the new artist," he said.

You can almost see weary working men and women gathered in dimly lit rooms, warmed by human contact, discussing a new piece of poetry. This translates not only to intellectual stimulation, but to friendship shared by people of all ages drawn together by like interests.

Holub shared the following poem. It is taken from *Miroslav Holub Although*, translated by Ian and Jarmila Milner:

> *Prague, January*
> *And here Picasso's bulls are stamping.*
> *And here Dali's elephants march on spider legs.*
> *And here Schonberg's drums are beating.*
> *And here the gentleman of La Mancha rides.*
> *And here the Karamazovs are carrying Hamlet.*
> *And here is the nucleus of the atom.*

And here is the lunar cosmodrome.
And here a statue stands without a torch.
And here the torch runs without the statue.
And it's plain. Where man
ends, flame begins.
And then in silence, you hear the chatter
of ash worms. Because
the millards of people mainly
keep their mouths shut.

Although the poem has far deeper meaning, it also illustrates that making friends is not about being silent. It's part of being human, concerned, assertive—alive! There's no shame in wanting friends. They are as necessary to our spirits as food is to our bodies. We can spread out our friendships as we place food on the table of a buffet-banquet; meat may be the main course, but it's pallid if there are no other choices. And just as the diner may or may not have one favorite dish, everyone doesn't have to be a "best friend."

We may sample a dish we've never tried before and find it much to our liking, as we may make a friend of a much different age or culture. We may savor the taste of another dish and go back for more, like the beginning of a friendship. We may stuff ourselves with one dish yet never try it again in our lives, as we sometimes share confidences in a fleeting friendship with a stranger we'll never see again.

Some foods we sample at the buffet become staples in our own lives long after the banquet. Some we taste but they really don't please our palates and we forget them. We get the recipes for some, take them home, and add our own ingredients. Sometimes we lose a recipe, but the memory of the original dish stays with us forever, enriching our lives.

In turn, we enrich others' lives by making our own special contribution to the buffet. Some will like it. Some won't—but that doesn't mean anything is wrong with the offering; people simply have different tastes. The important thing is, we have contributed to the buffet. We don't come empty-handed expecting to feast on the provisions of others.

It's a shared experience. The more we bring, the larger the buffet, and the bigger the celebration. Friendships are like a banquet. We participate by contributing ourselves, and enjoying what is placed before us.

And like a banquet, our friendships should be celebrated at every opportunity. Food nourishes our body, but friendship feeds our spirit and touches the marrow of our lives.

This book is about the feast of friendship, and how we, each in his or her own way, can contribute to the banquet.

2 FRIENDSHIPS COME IN ALL SIZES

. . . and everyone needn't be a "best" friend

Psychotherapist Shirley Harrison of Glendale, California, says when she asks clients how they go about developing friends, they come up blank. "They say there is no one at work, and they don't think neighbors want to become friends. The first step is just to start talking to people superficially, then deepen the conversation with more and more private subjects. Typically, the other person starts reciprocating. It is the gradually growing sharing of intimacies that forms friendships. The two people find each other feeling, and caring. It makes it real safe."

We meet potential friends nearly everywhere people gather: in our workplaces (business or volunteer), organizations, clubs, places of worship, neighborhoods, sporting events, social gatherings, tour groups and school.

Both men and women make many lifetime friends during military service. "An isolated condition like being in the military service gives people a sense of being bonded together," says Don Newman, writer and expert on James Boswell, 18th century Samuel Johnson biographer.

Newman recalls an ongoing friendship that began when he was in the service more than 20 years ago. "I must have met Daly right after my arrival at camp. It seemed like I already knew him. I was a rube from the hills of Pennsylvania, and he was considered sort of an eccentric. He had a sense of humor. Maybe that's why we got along." After the service one helped the other financially through col-

13

lege, they participated in each other's weddings, and they remain best friends today.

English professor and author Dana Brookins notes that for her, lasting friendships have developed through work on political campaigns, from a little-theater group, at a creative-writing class she taught, during a conference on writing children's books, from a letter written by another author who admired her work, at work, and through her grown children's friends.

"From every activity I've ever been involved in I've harvested at least one friend," says Brookins. "And once I get hold of one of these marvelous creatures, I never let him or her go. I guess the message here is to get involved. Nobody's going to leave a friend in a basket on your doorstep. Once one develops a friend the relationship needs nurturing and care. We must recognize that we are herding animals—that John Donne had it right when he said no one is an island. We *are* each other."

Brookins, like many interviewed, considers "support" one attribute of friendship. The same friends she met through so many different activities became her links with sanity after her daughter was killed by a drunken driver. "Sometimes I'm nearly overwhelmed by the loss," she says. "But friends sustain me; in their goodness and concern, they reaffirm for me that life has purpose."

Leah Hernandez, a homemaker who was recently widowed, echoes this same theme. She, too, met many friends through organizations, including the Tops Club (for dieters), and as a volunteer at a local hospital.

"Gosh, I have so many good friends, especially since Big Andy died," she says. "They have been so understanding of my loneliness. I know they will always be there for me, but in the same light, I will always be there for them."

Not only do old friends become nearer and dearer when we're down, but sometimes we're more receptive to making new friends during times of grief.

Phyllis Talasco recalls that after her divorce several years ago she struck up an acquaintance with a man clerk who worked at a store near the mobile home park where she lived. As it turned out, he lived in the same park.

"He was bright and a good conversationalist and I enjoyed his company," she says. "Then he said one evening, 'Before you get the wrong idea, I must tell you, I have a male companion who lives with me. I'm gay.' Well, it shocked and disappointed me, but we became friends anyway, and partied with other residents of the park. To top it all off, I went to his wedding in a gay church in Riverside, California. He invited others from the park, but I was the only straight person there."

Talasco acknowledges her prejudice before her acquaintance with this man, but says people enjoy more openness during a time of deep hurt, and that helps one's personal growth despite the pain. "It was a transitional period in my life when I was more receptive and sensitive to change. A few years before, I probably would have turned from him."

Ruth Dever, 80, says it isn't death and taxes we're assured of: "It's change. Those who roll with the changes are survivors," she says.

Change can mean breaking away from tried and true (sometimes tired and trite) habits so we can meet new people.

Karen Olden, a nurse in New Mexico, met one of her best friends during healing ceremonies at a Native American sweat lodge.

Artist Barbara Cunningham met one of her best friends at the first rehearsal of the Long Beach, California, Symphony Chorus. Marion Lapins, 75, met a lifetime friend on a golf course in Mexico. Beverly Looper says she made a best friend while putting on makeup backstage in a darkened theater. Don Rutledge made lifetime friends from an outlaw motorcycle group he rode with in his youth. Stormy Sandquist made a best friend when her car broke down in Texas.

Eric L. Robinson, a mechanical engineer in New Mexico, says being in the right place at the right time plays a part in making friends. That, however, means getting out so you can *be* in the right place at the right time, and it involves openness to possibilities.

TO FIND POTENTIAL FRIENDS

- Get involved at your house of worship.
- Volunteer your time to a political campaign, a program to help the homeless, a battered children's shelter, an environmental cause, etc.
- Take up a new sport.
- Join a walking group, or form one.
- Take a dance class.
- Write letters to stay in touch with distant friends.
- Get a part-time job if you're not employed.
- Frequent a local restaurant for breakfast or coffee breaks.
- Become active in your school's alumni organization.
- Go on group tours.
- Read the local newspaper to find out what's going on in your community.
- Attend local arts and crafts shows.
- Join or form a book discussion club.
- Get to know your neighbors.
- Join a community theater group.
- Join a support group.

As you become more active, though, don't expect instant close friends. We sometimes fail to turn acquaintances into friends because we don't allow enough time.

On the other hand, an effort at resurrecting a friendship, or persisting in one that just never takes off, is useless. We have to sense when to halt the attempt. "People sometimes go to class reunions thinking they are going to rekindle old friendships," says Harrison, "but find that some of the people involved are very different now. They try to reactivate a relationship, but they and the other person are in different spots. It can be sad for them, but they just have to let go."

A businesswoman says she recently got together with a woman she'd been very close to in another state soon after both had divorced. "All she did was complain. She came to visit with her new boyfriend. We went out to lunch and sort of caught up on things. Then we went back to my office and I was anxious for her to leave. We had nothing left in common. We had gone different ways."

We develop different types of friends and acquaintances. All serve as life's touchstones. Some pass briefly through our lives; some leave us chafed; some lift us up, then dash us to the ground. Some become lasting best friends.

Let friendship creep gently to a height; if it rushes to it, it may soon run itself out of breath.
—Thomas Fuller, 17th century divinity scholar

GROWING FRIENDSHIPS

Like the acorn growing into the oak tree, friendships grow slowly. *Unlike* the oak, however, friendships can have many different types of seeds.

• **Acquaintances:** Co-workers, former schoolmates, professional and business people we deal with, parents of our children's friends, friends of friends, people who belong to organizations we join, members of churches we attend: These are our acquaintances. Generally we like them, but don't exchange confidences with them. Yet any of these people may, eventually, become close friends. As one respondent said, "I make acquaintances easily; friendship takes development, sometimes over a period of years."

Psychologist Sally L. Mattson of Brattleboro, Vermont, says Americans all too often view friendships as expendable whereas in other cultures group behavior takes precedence over individualism. "We have the attitude that if my friends don't do it the way I like to do it, I will find other friends."

If we try imposing our own values on acquaintances with attitudes such as "I'd like you better if . . . ," acquaintances will never become friends.

Timing is important. You may feel drawn to someone at a time when he or she is involved in other activities or ventures, and you may feel you've been given the cold shoulder. Yet another time the person may be more ready to pursue development of a friendship with you. A woman I worked with in Girl Scouts many years ago became a good friend 20 years later when we were reintroduced. Our lives had changed dramatically over those years, and we actually had more in common than we had when we first met.

• **Group friends:** When we join or form a group so we can acquire friends, they serve as reinforcement for similar beliefs, hobbies, avocations or careers.

John Zonka of CDI Enterprises, a home-based computer business, recently helped form a computer-users group, BBUG (Big Bear User's Group) in the mountain community of Big Bear, California. Zonka didn't involve himself with the group for friendships, but to share information and help other computer-users who lack some of his expertise. "I hand out friendships very reluctantly. A friend is somebody that if I had a shirt on my back and he was cold and shivering, I'd give it to him. Giving unreservedly: That's what friendship is to me. I get upset when I receive letters in the mail that say, 'Dear Good Friend.' I'm not.''

On the other hand, when Zonka joined the Colorado Mountain Club so he could learn how to scale mountains, he made several close friends. ''When you share life-and-death situations with someone, you learn more about that person in the crucible of the situation than under normal circumstances. In some instances your life would depend on him or her, and you evaluate the person faster and more completely than you might other types of people you meet,'' he says.

English professor Tim O'Sullivan, who teaches at a two-year commuter college, says students tell him they have no time for friendships once they get into college. ''They're busy studying, working part-time jobs and getting to and from school. They're looking for that group they had in high school—that whole gang like the Coca Cola crowd we see on television—but they just don't have time,'' he says. So styles of friendship change for people in all age groups.

• **Networking:** Networking serves many purposes, including friendship. As our socializing methods change, more people combine work and pleasure so they can make time for both. In today's busy world networking can serve as a substitute for traditional social gatherings.

Gail Kawanami Allen of Santa Ana, California, developer of Life Works Consulting Services, organized a close-knit group of people involved in transformational/spiritual work who network as they socialize. ''We interact on multiple levels, and close friendship is one of them,'' she says.

Allen, a former traditional psychotherapist, says she eventually realized structures inherent in conventional psychotherapy no longer held an appeal for her. So she decided on a more universal/holistic approach. She trains people to attract friends with similar creative energies using meditative rather than cognitive approaches. ''Networking is one of our biggest growing sources of friendships,'' she says. "Most people's friends come from work today, so they don't go out as much anymore just to meet people. Attracting people who accept me for who and what I am, and vice-versa, requires integrating the right and left brains."

We usually initially choose friends based on what they say and their behavior. Allen believes getting past traditional methods involves visualizing a person's energy thought forms, and is more important than cognitive feedback. "We are attracted to people who are healthy in thought. By tapping into their energy, we get past superficiality and into their spiritual nature," she says. Allen promotes friendships through networks of people interested in healing themselves through a conscious life filled with empowerment of self and one incorporating global transformation.

Another networking method takes place among established friends or acquaintances. For example, Hollywood scriptwriter Creighton Barnes recalls that during college, a professor eyed the dozen or so people in a scriptwriting class. "Make friends with everyone in this room," he admonished. "At least two of you will make it big. Those two eventually call their friends when other jobs open at the studios."

"That's exactly what happened," Barnes recalls. "Years later, a friend from class called and said the company he worked for needed writers for a new television cartoon series. That's how I got my foot in the door." He's still writing for the studios from that one tip-off.

We can't work in a vacuum. Take writing, perceived as a lonely profession. Many writers enjoy isolation. Yet if we remain alone too long we get stale, because the world changes constantly. We bounce ideas off one another, garnering bits and pieces from all our contacts, writers or no. We can't write inventively if we don't associate with people from all walks of life.

A nationally known educator discussing the need for reading skills once said how awful it must be for a person who can't read the writing of history's great thinkers. Nonreaders are stuck for life with only their own thoughts and ideas. People who don't mingle with others, who only associate with people who think as they do, stagnate.

We limit possible friendships when we confine ourselves to those who think, act and dress just as we do. It stunts our growth, retards our thinking.

• **Spiritual fellowship:** In addition to spiritual enrichment, places of worship often open a door to lasting friendships. Fellowship, defined as a mutual sharing among people of like interests, and friendship, defined as attachment between friends, differ. We can meet potential friends through fellowship, however, and friendship might follow.

Zonka gives high marks to people he recently met when he began attending church after a long absence. "They seem to provide more love and care than the general populace. Acquaintances I've made at church could eventually become friends."

Unitarian minister Ellen Livingston of Claremont, California, acknowledges that many people start attending church specifically for companionship. "And that's okay," she says. "Where better to meet people with common interests? Going to a place of worship doesn't guarantee instant friendships. It does, however, provide a comfortable setting in which to begin friendships because commonalities exist among those who attend."

• **Comrades or confederates:** People with whom we might share something in common—a hobby, work, service on a committee, age or support group—become comrades or confederates. They might present themselves at a particular support group such as a weight-loss or Alcoholic's Anonymous meeting. People with shared experiences may become close friends, but often they just become casual acquaintances after completing, canceling, or outgrowing an activity.

We sometimes wonder what happened to friends we made at

work when we left for another job. We might keep in contact with them during holidays, but the best-friend status is lost. Sharing work isn't like sharing feelings, which are a mainstay of close friendships. Then too, many people prefer to keep their work and personal lives separate.

• **Helping friends:** Temporary friendships can develop between a strong group member and someone who relies on that person. This type of friendship often ends when the weak one becomes stronger. Unhealthy friendships can develop from this structure. Some people thrive on being the healthy one because they can feel superior to the one needing help.

Illustrations of strong/weak relationships abound. For example, Harrison, who treats agoraphobia, defined as a "fear of open spaces," says when agoraphobics begin to overcome some fears and assert themselves, their spouses often rebel because they see their safe, controlling environments threatened; frequently the marriage ends.

One the other hand, she says, "I've seen people go through situations where they've had serious trauma, and certain people helped them through it. When the victim gets to the trauma's other side, he or she doesn't want to deal with those who gave support anymore, consciously or unconsciously choosing not to relive the bad period. It's very sad when this happens because the person can lose potential quality relationships. Those who helped could have grown with the person, and they could have developed different types of friendships."

• **Neighbors:** We become nostalgic when we think about small towns. Most people today live in urban areas, places seemingly callous and uncaring, sometimes even dangerous. Weeks may pass before we even get chances for neighborly hellos on our way to or from work. Media reports, however, show families by the thousands moving back to small towns so they can reestablish connection with more intimate communities. I moved to a town of about 500 people 12 years ago following a divorce, and I remember the slight movements of curtains in my new neighbors' homes as they peeked out at my furniture-laden truck bumping over dirt roads back to my cabin. It alarmed me; I saw their curiosity as nosiness. Yet eventually I too watched when unfamiliar vehicles came down the road, and that's part of a small town's coziness. Further, when you know everyone, and know the happenings in your immediate neighborhood, crime goes down. That's what Neighborhood Watch programs are all about.

The program has thrived in some areas, just as the practice of making neighbors friends can thrive. Though I no longer live there, I still cherish my good friends from that small town, and we stay in contact by phone or letter.

Several people I interviewed said neighbors became best friends over the years. One woman who moved from Indiana to Florida when her husband retired says her neighbors became great friends when her husband had surgery. They had only spoken casually before that, but when she had problems getting to and from the hospital because she didn't drive, the neighbors offered to take her, opening the door to close friendships.

• **Best Friends:** These come in all sizes, ages and backgrounds, not necessarily sharing all our interests, although a few commonalities might bond us.

Bette Ross describes the process of turning an acquaintance into a best friend as "falling in like." Some people prefer the term "close" to "best." One woman said she resented drawing an imaginary line anywhere on degrees of friendship since friendships vary in intensity.

Dana Brookins says particular occasions call for specialness among her best friends. She therefore treats the person she's with as someone special—a skill developed by people with many friends. One person she calls a best friend goes gambling with her in Las Vegas. Yet she shares a love for theater with another person, and "When we drive into Los Angeles to see a play, we're best friends all during that trip.''

The need for a ''best'' friend develops in youngsters, who often require mutual exclusivity. In adulthood, however, ''Different friends meet different needs and share their own special companionship,'' Bookins says.

Many people say a spouse, a brother or sister is their best friend, and some women say their children, particularly daughters, have become their best friends after becoming adults. ''I consider my sister, Lois, my best friend,'' one woman told me. ''She more than anyone knows my failures. She is five years younger than I, so our time growing up was not always friendly. It took years before that five-year gap narrowed enough for us to become real friends—I guess it wasn't until after we both married and had children. The older we get, the closer we are. She can always make me laugh when I'm down. We're alike, but different. She wrote a poem about us for my birthday that I'll always cherish. She calls it 'Genes.'''

> *I like camping*
> *She likes to bowl*
> *I like the outdoors*
> *She likes malls*
>
> *I like to walk in the snow*
> *She likes to crochet*
>
> *We both like to laugh*
> *We're sisters!!*

One man, a liberal writer and author of suspense novels, says his brother, who is a policeman, is his best friend. ''Although our ideas about politics, equal rights, etcetera are as different as night and day, there is a core set of values we are in tune with. I can always go to him and he takes me in, with all my problems.''

Clearly, the idea of best friends is laced with a variety of meanings for different people. We interact with best, intimate, close or choice friends for several reasons and purposes. Most of us don't try to acquire a great many best friends. A few are all we need.

Our attitudes about best friends continually change as we age. Stormy Sandquist says, "I used to think one person would be all things in friendship, but in my early 30s I realized this was unrealistic, that having a variety of friends with a variety of interests works out better. So there are people we can discuss politics with, others we go to flea markets with, some who share our gardening interests, others who share our concerns for nature and conservation. No one person will have *all* the same interests we have. The best you can hope for are three or four shared interests. Neither should the fact that you disagree on two or three matters ruin a friendship. Just agree to disagree on those issues—unless there are major things that go entirely against your value system; then it doesn't work. Or if the relationship is bad for your health. Also, a person shouldn't go somewhere or do something he or she isn't particularly interested in just to make friends. It never works."

Best friends give us latitude. We're free to do nothing when we're with them.

And "Good friends become even better with time," says Paula Emick, an elementary school teacher.

Several people mentioned particular qualities they admire in best friends. No one possesses them all, of course, but they show what people look for in others. Not one person listed money, and a sense of humor topped the list.

QUALITIES IN FRIENDSHIPS

Those interviewed said they seek a good friend who:

Has a sense of humor
Is trustworthy
Has listening skills
Is sensitive
Is open-minded
Is reliable
Is honest with others, including about feelings
Is inner-directed
Is independent
Is understanding
Has principles
Is loyal
Has patience
Is considerate and caring
Is nonbigoted
Has tact
Is forgiving
Has a variety of interests
Can share emotional as well as intellectual concerns
Is comfortable to be with
Is willing to exchange ideas
Is willing to share problems
Will help when help is needed
Has a strong sense of fairness
Accepts you as you are
Rejoices at your good fortune, grieves at your misfortune
Isn't jealous
Doesn't put you down for your ideas
Shares similar interests
Sees beyond your flaws
Believes in humanity
Is willing to think about your interests

Respects your right to your own opinion
Has similar values
Is interested in the world

Reading this list, one might think it takes sainthood to be a friend, but these qualities represent the ideal. One woman said emphatically that a good friend is "someone who puts up with me when I do stupid things." Yet we can consider these attributes as we evaluate our own characters. Friendship begins with us.

THE HAPPINESS FACTOR

Happiness, too, begins with the individual, and friendship plays a role in that happiness.

Ruth B. Weg, former professor of gerontology at the University of Southern California's Leonard Davis School of Gerontology. says friendships are crucial to happiness in middle and later years, making it imperative that we hang onto our long-time friends because making friends becomes much harder as we age.

"What we really should do is teach children the importance of friendships, but we don't. If we could begin early enough [teaching the skills of friendship], we wouldn't have such problems as we mature," she says.

Happiness in friendships, though, is a double-edged sword. Just *having* friends doesn't do the trick, although that is part of it. Being happy in the first place attracts friends. Alice M. Isen, who is associated with the Samuel Curtis Johnson Graduate School of Management and is a professor of psychology at Cornell University, says that when people are happy, they are more cooperative and sociable with others and see less distinction between themselves and others. "They see themselves as parts of a larger whole."

The supreme happiness of life is the conviction that we are loved.
—Victor Hugo, *Les Miserables*, 1862

HOW TO MAKE FRIENDS

Laurence Grimm, clinical psychologist and professor at the University of Illinois, Chicago, agrees. "Unfortunately some people have never learned how to make friends. They either are rejected by their peers because they're obnoxious, or they just don't know how. They stay somewhat isolated going through stressful periods alone. We can convince them they need social support, but then we have to teach them how to get it.

"Certain dysfunctional beliefs about relationships inhibit our willingness to change our thinking about what it takes to develop them. Also, our beliefs and attitudes about other issues can hinder development of relationships," he adds.

If problems continually erupt during friendship development, two broad areas need scrutiny:

1. Have you the skill required to meet people in the first place?
2. Have you the skill to move from the first meeting to a deeper relationship?

The first involves making yourself attractive as a person, but not just physically. Recognize your good qualities and learn to like yourself. "Once you truly like yourself, it becomes rather effortless to meet new people," says Grimm.

The second skill needed to move a budding friendship along requires reciprocal self-disclosure. People test others, often unconsciously, to see how they will react. We might disclose an embarrassing event in our lives, waiting for a reaction. If the other person appears judgmental or critical, a blossoming friendship might stop right there. If the person is sympathetic, responding with something like "That must have been difficult for you," or tells a similar story about himself or herself, it builds trust. "People are very attuned to this kind of disclosure," says Grimm.

On the other hand, people can disclose personal facts too soon, making others uncomfortable. The listener becomes cautious. People are often labeled weird if they disclose at the wrong rate, according to Grimm.

And some people don't disclose anything about themselves, coming across as distant.

A friendship develops like a chess game, with different strategies governing each stage, says Grimm. Stage one: What do we have in common? Stage two: How much can I trust you? Stage three: I don't have to be on my best behavior.

First, a person must determine if he or she really wants friends. Says Grimm: "Some people give off vibes like they want friends, but they really don't. It's like overweight people who come in for therapy saying they want to lose weight, when that isn't really what they want at all. One woman came in saying she wanted to lose weight, but in reality she liked to use her weight as a sign of hostility toward her husband. And there are people who say they want friends, but who really don't. They're afraid to trust and have a relationship."

On the other hand, some people don't *need* many friends. Introverts can be happy with just one or two good friends.

"The big problem comes when people are sincere about wanting friends and are unable to make them," says Grimm. These people usually recognize an existing problem. It may stem from early childhood. Perhaps the parents acted anxious about friendships. Too, some dysfunctional families view relationships outside the family as betrayal. "Children from these families often feel guilty when they make outside friends, and this spills over into adulthood," Grimm explains.

People who grew up in military families often struggle making friends. "As children they learned to make friends only on a superficial level because they moved so often. Even when they get settled as adults, that pattern is so deeply ingrained it's hard to change," says Grimm.

Mary Swaney, who grew up in a military family, acknowledges that making friends still entails problems. She can remember no friends from her youth. "I was afraid to get too close to people."

Now, she says, "I make myself too open and it seems to scare people. They shy away. When I try to close off a little, the same thing happens."

In the past ten years, however, she acquired three of the best friends she's ever known. One friendship began after she took a part-time job. "At first we didn't get along at all. We were both part-timers and probably were in competition with one another for a full-time position. Then one evening she asked me if I liked Superman movies. We watched one together and have been friends ever since. Of course the enduring friendship took years to mature, and we've been through tragedies, so we've grown together."

Swaney says of friendship: "If a true friendship can be found, cherish it like a fine gem. Polish it, go out of your way to keep and protect it. Keep it safe, but let it shine for itself. It will grow and grow."

DO'S AND DON'TS FOR GETTING BETTER ACQUAINTED

DO

- Accept and give gifts joyfully
- Reciprocate favors
- Share activities you both enjoy
- Be a mentor, or accept another as a mentor

- Be yourself
- Express your feelings
- Be direct and honest, but tactful
- Practice integrity and affirm your values
- Try to understand the other person
- Take the blame when you deserve it
- Seek the advice of others
- Accept change
- Work out compromises in touchy situations
- Trust others—and trust yourself
- Be forgiving of yourself *and* others
- Accept a friend's faults as well as his or her good points

DON'T

- Place limits on your friends
- Practice one-upmanship
- Be pushy
- Limit friendships to your own age group
- Try to place blame on others
- Insist on always having your way
- Become too dependent on others
- Try to always have the answer to everything
- Expect too much from a friend
- Make excuses for your own poor behavior
- Agree with everything others say or do
- Be afraid to say "no"

3 MEN DON'T MAKE CLOSE FRIENDS

. . . and other myths

DIFFERENCES IN MALE AND FEMALE FRIENDSHIPS

Author and student Bill Carney answered the question "What is your best experience with a friend?" by saying, "Sounds silly, but one time my friend John came over just to sit and talk. Most people don't come over just to spend time like that. Usually, it's to go do other things and we'll talk while we're doing those things."

In another instance, the former wife of a man who had difficulty making friends said that after their divorce, her ex made friends with a golfing companion and the man's wife. Some time later he told her the man had died, and how sorry he felt about losing the friendship. She asked if he'd gone to see the widow to tell her about his sadness at his friend's death. The former husband replied that it wasn't necessary, since the man was dead and gone and the wife didn't golf.

This story is an extreme example of how we perceive the traditional male way of dealing with friendships. Men usually *do* something when they're spending time with a friend. As Carney points out, some men can just sit and talk without an activity. Even so, he suggests that intimate talk between men is rare.

We often judge intimacy from a female perspective. We perceive that it involves self-disclosure, sharing many details about oneself, and reviewing problems. But it seems gender-specific—a female thing.

33

"We tend to think of friendship one-dimensionally based on women's identification of it," says Lawrence Frey, associate professor of communications at Loyola University, Chicago, and author of *Investigating Communication: Introduction to Research Methods.* "Traditionally, men's friendships involve establishing confidences and women's involve establishing connections.

"We equate sharing with self-disclosure. Yet there are key differences in what is going on in these relationships. There are different modes of friendship," he says.

AGENTIC AND COMMUNAL MODES OF FRIENDSHIP

Frey referred to studies by Bill Rawlins of Purdue University identifying two different modes of communication: agentic and communal. The agentic mode works toward accomplishment of a task or goal. The communal mode is based on sharing and usually happens between women.

Although the agentic mode is more psychologically male and the communal mode more psychologically female, neither has anything to do with physical gender.

"There are lots of men who would fall into the communal mode because they happen to be feminine in their psychological orientation. Men who readily share more in relationships have higher rates of male-female androgynous characteristics. Yet it has nothing to do with their maleness," says Frey.

A recent study by Gerald P. Jones, an affiliated scholar at the University of Southern California's Institute for the Study of Women and Men in Society, suggests male-female androgynous characteristics show up in adolescence.

Jones' studies cast doubt on previous research among children and adults that always showed females scoring higher than males in the ability to develop intimate friends. His studies show the determining factor in friendship intimacy hinging on how people perceived their gender roles, whether male or female.

"My study showed that the sex role is more important in determining who can and can't make friends, and that genitalia alone don't determine how men and women make friends," says Jones.

Boys who scored high on both male and female traits, according to their self-perceptions, also scored as high as girls on self-perceptions of friendship intimacy. Boys who didn't score as high had greater stereotypically macho self-images. If future studies back this research, adult males who accept some positive elements of traditional female roles may have an easier time moving back and forth between agentic and communal modes of friendship.

"We need to do the same type of research, but with four instead of two categories," Jones says. This would include male and female, as well as androgynous male and female psychological types. "The question then becomes, is there a correlation between androgynous males and males who are more intimate with their friends?" he says.

Jones believes roles people play in society tell us more than we can learn solely from their male or female physiology.

We need to respect male-type intimacy, because it frees us to march between male and female types of friendships to the beat of our own drums. Self-revelation and disclosure are great if that's a person's style, but there are other roads to friendships.

WE NEED DIFFERENT STYLES OF FRIENDSHIPS

"Men use activities with other men as an escape from the daily pressures of dealing with their work and environment problems," says Frey. "When they have problems with relationships, however, they often turn to women. Women are more oriented toward those things to begin with, and we rely on them. We rely on different people for different needs.

"People are very complex and these different sides emerge when we interact with friends. It's not an issue of good or bad, but of differences. Men need male friendships to escape the daily grind. Men look for escape, not problem-solving, in their talk with other men."

Male-to-male communication, different from that between women, still presents a form of caring, connection and relying on others for support, according to Frey. "It's not the typical way we look at friendships. Men share, but not about men things. Men have a deeper sense of privacy about self; women are much more open about details. Men don't get into that, although some are very expressive and feeling-oriented," he says.

Frey believes it's important for men to get together with their buddies. "We all escape in some ways, and these escapes provide some gound for us to recoup our energy and resources. Men treat their male relationships like vacations."

Women are also beginning to link activity with friendships. Many find it as comforting to meet after work for a five-mile walk as to meet for lunch to share work problems. An activity may provide a needed escape from the pressures and responsibilities of work, once considered the bastion of men. "It's a matter of women trying to experience more of the other side to meet their needs. Basically I get the feeling that people believe they can't be happy unless they do X. That seems to ignore individual needs, and individuals are the best judges of what those are," says Frey.

For example, if a man wants more intimacy in a friendship; if a woman chooses more activity-oriented social gatherings: Both should feel free to follow personal dictates.

"A lot of what we term friendship is contextually based. We need different things from different friendships. There are many women I wouldn't ask about personal relationships. There are others I would.

It's an individual thing. Some men I talk to more about problems than others. The one thing we try to teach is that there isn't only one way of communicating. People who believe there is use very simplistic formulas. That's true in friendships as well. It really depends on personal style," says Frey.

"I've had good friends over the years, but never talked about serious problems with them," says college professor Tim O'Sullivan. "I remember one best friend; we were in the service together. When we got out he needed some money for college. I forced the money on him, and he reluctantly took it. When his mustering-out pay came he tried to give it all to me, even though he had lots of debts to pay off. That was the kind of friend he was. When I needed help, he was always there for me, too. Later, as our lives changed, we saw one another on occasion and talked about the past, but it wasn't the same. We had moved into different worlds."

MEN NEED INTIMACY

Paul Lee, licensed clinical social worker at the Men's Resource Center in Portland, Oregon, says men come in wanting friendships, especially after a divorce. "For a lot of guys it's disorienting because they don't appreciate the important role good male friends can play in their lives. They go from living in their parental families to college to marriage, and don't expect to establish male friendships. They don't realize that having male friends can be a part of adult life. They need to learn two things: first, that male friends can be important, and second, how to find friends that can be reliable, trustworthy and intimate.

"Men tend to meet through activities like sports and drinking, which aren't conducive to intimacy."

Lee says he tries to help men break down barriers to intimacy by challenging them to start doing things outside their regular habits. "As children, boys make friends through activities. It's the model boys learn, along with seeing movie and television stereotypes of the quiet, stoic male—the John Wayne syndrome. All this leads to isolation."

Men can train themselves to use words like "I feel," instead of "I think," to break isolation barriers and get in touch with their emotions. A man can practice this alone, and once he's in touch with his feelings, communicating honestly with others becomes much easier.

WE LEARN FRIENDSHIP STYLES FROM OUR FAMILIES

Besides androgynous roles, research shows men learn from the way their parental families dealt with friendships.

For example, the wife of Nick Livingston, an architect, credits him with unusual friendmaking abilities. "He is rare in his friendships," she says.

Livingston, in turn, credits his family, saying his father was a "charming, humorous guy," and his mother "like a corporate head, organizing parties all the time."

He was an only child, so Livingston learned to reach out to friends to make up for the lack of brothers and sisters. He speaks fondly about a family he knew in Chicago who all extended friendship. "Maybe I started out being friends with one member, but I got to know the whole family. I was involved with everyone. I was friends with their kids and their siblings and their parents."

Friendships, then, crossed all barriers: including age and sex— because he had female friends within the family whom he valued as much as the male ones.

Yet Livingston acknowledges his initial contact involved men, and that when just the men got together, they followed activity-oriented formats that involved poker games, jogging, sports.

"We would talk about serious things, but in a round-about way. We weren't a therapy group, but through the years you pick up where someone is coming from. With men, maybe it's like doing therapy with children. It's oblique. It can be based on what someone *doesn't* say," he says.

Certain types of friendships offer no revelations. Tim O'Sullivan says he came from a big Irish family, so he never saw much need to cultivate outside friendships and, he acknowledges, he still doesn't. His family never entertained many outsiders, which he believes may have kept him from developing intimate outside friendships as he grew older.

Recalls O'Sullivan: "I spent three years with this fella, another instructor, at a school in Pasadena, California. I used to have lunch with him. Dinner occasionally. Toward the end of our first year, some students asked me if the man was married. I had to tell them I didn't know. At the end of the third year they asked if he had kids, and I didn't know. I'd gone sailing and all sorts of other places with him, but I didn't really know anything about him."

Still, they had a friendship. Maybe not one considered "intimate" in the communal sense, yet it filled the male need to escape, to regroup. O'Sullivan isn't considered a cold person; co-workers say he's one of the most popular professors on campus, and that he's a wonderful friend to many.

THE LAUGHTER FACTOR

The banter involved in comedy and storytelling is another characteristic of male friendships. "Men are simply better at it than women because those activities are considered a form of power. Traditionally, women have shied away from this type of power. Maybe because it draws too much attention to oneself," says Frey.

Women may not tell as many jokes or funny stories, but they laugh more than men, according to Lucille Nahemow, professor of family studies and a specialist on aging at the University of Connecticut. "Most of us, male and female, are too uptight most of the time," she says.

On the other hand, just as some men are knocking down barriers to intimacy, women are coming to terms with what we perceive as power. There is evidence of this in the number of female comedians on the airwaves and at comedy clubs. Yet humor, as a natural part of daily living, is a problem for both genders. Natural humor in conversation seems rarer today than in the past, according to many health professionals.

"In prehistoric times people laughed all the time," says Matt Weinstein, health professional and president of Playfair Inc., a Berkeley, California, company that gives seminars devoted to lightening up the workplace.

"The child inside of us is really what's human in us. We allow our children to behave in open, loving ways, but that stops at a certain age when we think it becomes unacceptable," says Weinstein. "Technology brings with it a need for humor, laughter and play."

A sense of humor and laughter promote social interaction, improving our psychological sense of well-being, according to William Fry, M.D., professor of clinical psychiatry, Stanford University Medical Center. He says we should no longer consider humor a trivial or inconsequential part of our lives.

Alice M. Isen, psychology professor at Cornell University, says jokes have a profound effect on the ways we act, think, and treat each other. "Humor is one way to induce positive feelings," she says. "Humor that is nonhostile and nonsexual also facilitates creative problem-solving in negotiation and integrative bargaining. With it people can achieve not only a better outcome but the best possible outcome."

In control groups that bargain face to face, most people eventually stop before reaching an agreement. Yet if given a free gift or cartoon of a nonsexual, nonhostile nature, they are more likely to reach an agreement that provides the best payoff for both parties, according to Isen. "Humor also has a positive effect on creativity, social interaction, altruism, and helping."

Results of four studies Isen conducted on creativity showed positive effects from a comedy film or small piece of candy. Elation, if it involves arousal, seems to help people solve problems requiring ingenuity or innovation.

Even when a problem seems insurmountable, humor helps the situation, says Nahamow. "Aging people have a humor about the underdog. It brings them together and points out uncomfortable situations people are in. It creates a sense of ridiculousness at how society puts down older people, especially older women."

We use humor to seek approval, according to J. J. M. Askenasy, Department of Neurology, Tel-Aviv School of Medicine in Israel, who says in the *Journal of General Psychology* that sometimes laughter enhances self-confidence and dissipates uncertainty in human contact. When one person tells a joke and the other laughs, it renews the certainty of the contact. Laughter binds people together.

Livingston recalled one man in a long-time group of friends who had a superb sense of humor. "Malcolm never talked about his feelings, but he was incredibly witty—as funny as any stand-up comedian you'd find in Las Vegas. He never made a nasty remark about anyone. But through his humor he revealed a great deal about himself."

Livingston's friend knew the secret of true humor. He didn't make fun of others. Experts agree that positive humor—laughing *with*, rather than *at*, people—turns others on.

A merry heart doeth good like a medicine. But a broken spirit dryeth the bones.

—Proverbs 17:22

MALE/FEMALE FRIENDS ARE POSSIBLE, BUT . . .

Until the late 1960s, male-female friendships were rare. Then, mostly because of changing work habits, more platonic relationships began to develop. Even today, however, single men and women have more freedom in opposite-sex friendships than married people. Subtle parameters still exist for married couples.

Ellen Livingston recalls a couple she counseled—an American man who married a Filipino woman. The woman had been engaged before coming to the United States, and she kept in close touch with her former fiancée by phone after her marriage. Meanwhile, her husband also kept in touch with a co-worker in New York by phone. Since both wife and husband had been intimately involved with the people they now considered friends, it put a strain on the marriage.

Livingston herself had made a friend of a former boyfriend following her marriage. But her husband found that acceptable since the friendship included him. "It's better if the third person becomes a friend of the couple's, not just of the one partner."

Although Livingston doesn't consider the boyfriend her best friend, some people interviewed said former mates are now their best friends. Zoltan Mate, 77, says, "I have this gal I've known for a long spell. We are closer today than when we lived together. Of course, that's because things have changed. She visits and would come if I needed her. Even her husband approves of our relationship."

Another woman recalls that many years ago, when she was struggling with some problems in her marriage, a therapist advised her to resist having lunch alone with a male friend. Some people didn't consider it proper in the 1950s, she says.

Today, as a single woman, she enjoys many male friendships.

Bette Ross says that although she considered several married friends' husbands good friends, their wives wouldn't allow them to become best friends outside a couple relationship. As a married woman herself, she understands. "I don't honestly know that closer association wouldn't lead to sexual interests."

When a single person makes a best friend of a married person of the opposite sex, problems can evolve. Bill Carney, a single man, says best friends of the opposite sex always interest him sexually, whether or not he acts on it. "I always have sexual feelings about women. It's a biological thing. But I do have good women friends with whom I have no sex."

Paul Lee, of the Men's Resource Center, says: "Personally I have friendships with women to whom I'm not sexually attracted. With others there is a sexual energy we know is there, but we choose not to act on it."

Lee, who's married, says his wife knows he has women friends, knows an attraction could exist, but manages her feelings about it through trust. "She has friends of the opposite sex, but there's no jealousy because there's no sexual interest. If there were, I would have a hard time respecting that. For the most part I'm friends with her male friends, and my wife has met my female friends. She knows them all slightly. They are women I know through a musical group I play in. We get together a few times a week, but she doesn't have much of a relationship with them."

Lee points out the deep friendships between many gay men and lesbians, and also between straight women and gay men. "Many gay men, not all necessarily, have already broken down a lot of macho stereotypes. They have more experience in being intimate than straight men. My guess is that when you drop the straight-man stereotype it's liberating; and women, both single and married, find it easy to develop intimate friendships with gay men," he says.

THE DANGER OF PLATONIC RELATIONSHIPS

Platonic friendships that become affairs interest Baltimore, Maryland, psychologist Shirley Glass, who studies and writes about the subject extensively.

A married man is more apt to become intimate with a female friend than a married woman is with a male friend, Glass says. Yet both are vulnerable, especially if they talk negatively to one another about their primary relationships. "They often say they were aware of the good friendship, but weren't aware it was turning into something more. In therapy the partners often come in and say they are jealous of a spouse's friendship," she says. "Some therapists will blame it on the person coming in, and not give credence to the fact that it is a legitimate concern. Just because people aren't having sex, that doesn't mean it's not an affair."

Three elements of platonic relationships between married people and opposite-sex friends can cause damage to a marriage: (1) secrecy, (2) chemistry, and (3) emotional intimacy.

"Even if people aren't having sex, if they're talking about it there is a level of emotional involvement," says Glass. "If the person is turning to someone of the opposite sex outside the marriage for emotional intimacy, it presents a danger to the marriage."

When a man suspects his wife of having an affair, he usually will ask, "Did you have sex?" A woman, if she thinks her husband has been unfaithful, often asks about emotional involvement, says Glass. "Men have more difficulty sharing emotions with another man, so they turn to a woman. Women can easily turn to a same-sex friend to share emotions."

Glass believes having sex often ruins a good friendship. "It changes expectations. So if a person is going into a relationship he or she should seriously evaluate it, because it's easy to find a lover, but hard to find a good friend," she says, adding that when people are working together professionally and get involved emotionally, it can ruin the working relationship.

PROBLEMS WITH SAME-SEX FRIENDS

Same-sex friends also can present problems to married couples. Sometimes a man becomes jealous of his partner's close association with another woman, believing they confide in one another too deeply. A woman, too, sometimes resents her husband's buddies.

"I had that in my first marriage," says Ellen Livingston. "He sat around the house a lot drinking with buddies and staying out until all hours. It was unsettling, and I was somewhat jealous. I saw it as a threat."

Her second husband said he understands because he had been the one to hang out with buddies too much in his first marriage. He had an early-morning tennis game with a buddy every Saturday. That fostered hostility in his wife because she preferred to stay in bed snuggling with her mate.

Men traditionally get together for such activities as baseball games. Rare is the statement from a woman, "I'm going to the ballgame with Annie."

Yet this tradition, too, is changing as the friendship roles among men and women take new forms.

These forms aren't set in concrete. Friendship isn't like a marriage or a business agreement. No structure need exist, and rules are nebulous. Psychotherapist Lillian Rubin writes in *Just Friends* that friendship is a private affair. It "just becomes." Ray Bradbury, author of dozens of novels, stories, plays and poems, reminds us in *Zen in the Art of Writing: Essays on Creativity*, "Who are your friends? Do they believe in you? Or do they stunt your growth with ridicule and disbelief: If the latter, you haven't friends. Go find some."

GOSSIP ISN'T ALL BAD

William Least Heat-Moon, author of *Prairy Erth*, quotes a woman living in a small Kansas prairie town: ''We have limits, of course. The first and most powerful enforcement is gossip and scorn, the sap and sinew of a small town.''

Certain types of gossip, rather than being idle wastings of a flapping mouth, find a place in friendships, since friendship involves communication.

Psychologist Lois Langland says nonmalicious gossip provides a cathartic release, and sometimes prevents us from needlessly jeopardizing a basically sound relationship.

For example, suppose a friend runs around on his wife, and this disturbs you to the point that you confront him about his actions. He says it's none of your business. You're hurt, but rather than end the friendship since he has many qualities you admire and respect, you turn to another friend to vent your frustrations about the unfaithful husband's behavior. You thus deal with your negative feelings in a more constructive way than if you continue to harangue the philandering husband.

It's important, though, to tell a good, trusting friend who won't use the information maliciously. ''I personally will never gossip to anyone who will use the information harmfully. Sometimes we need to tell something to get it off our chest if we're having a hard time keeping still about it,'' says Langland.

Gossip can also serve a protective function. Suppose a neighbor tells you she believes the man next door beats his wife, who happens to be a friend of yours. You're shocked, but confront the wife. The story, if true, allows you to suggest that she seek help and leave the abusive situation.

''It's part of a communication network that can be helpful,'' says Langland. ''I suppose in that sense it depends on your motivation.''

Small towns operate this way. Certain behaviors aren't acceptable. People shun those who don't adhere to the standards set by their fellow townspeople. This provides a way to say, "Shape up or ship out." Primitive tribes use like methods. Someone who steals from another won't be sent to prison, but instead finds him- or herself completely ignored, maybe for years.

The son of an African tribal chief, Opoku, educated in London and now living and working in California, once told me, "In my country, if someone is evil or a thief or treats his or her family badly, we consider him or her a non-person. We ignore him or her as if he or she didn't exist. To the person this is worse than jail, and to be accepted again he or she must make amends. Our way inspires a person to change."

And if they don't change? I asked.

"They have a poor funeral. When someone dies the entire village chips in for the funeral. The better thought of the person, the more offered. This way a person's entire life is judged. But though the person isn't regarded highly, we still see to it that he or she has a decent burial. The person, after all, is a part of us."

Another form of gossip, considered by some the most malicious, involves yellow journalism, or tabloid trite. Few people acknowledge buying these periodicals at the market checkout stands, yet the average weekly circulation of the five leading tabloids combined hovers above 11 million.

Langland believes tabloids prey on people's need to be mean. "We all have that capacity, but we work to train ourselves so we don't have it. In reality, Americans don't talk enough to one another. Not that gossip is necessary, but talking more with friends might lessen the need for malicious gossip."

Langland indentifies malicious gossip as "that which is spread for the purpose of causing people to be hurt—to suffer humiliation or serious damage to their reputations."

We're curious about others' lifestyles. When I worked as a reporter, editors always insisted we get the person's age whether it was pertinent to the story or not. Editors explain that readers like to compare themselves with the people written about. If a 60-year-old has just bicycled cross-country, and we just turned 60, it may lift our spirits to know we too could attempt such a venture. On the other hand, it could make us feel like lazy slugs. A newspaper article that details a new trade agreement with Japan would seem boring without a description of the representatives who signed it. Did their hands shake when they held the pen? Did anyone break out in a sweat?

Without gossip we never would have learned about Watergate, what really caused the Love Canal pollution, or how Native Americans lost their lands. We get more to the truth of matters when we hear how government machinations affect others. Paper-trails don't give us the full story. Footprints do.

So how do we discern between "good" gossip and that considered malicious? We may simply need to examine our motivations. Langland believes people who spread malicious gossip need to reassure themselves and others they are people of value. They are attempting to prove their worth by denying the worth of others.

Malicious gossip doesn't sit well in friendship circles.

I hold it to be a fact, that if all persons knew what each said of the other, there would not be four friends in the world.
—Blaise Pascal, 17th century French
mathematician and philosopher

4 FRIENDSHIP IS GOOD MEDICINE

. . . and not hard to swallow, with or without sugar

REACHING OUT

It's never too late to develop friendships that work best for you—whether in groups or one on one. In today's changing culture, with extended families no longer filling our needs, stretching a hand out to support groups, volunteer organizations and other individuals helps us stay healthy in body, mind and spirit.

Medical research shows that social isolation is a major health-risk factor. In a 1985 article in *Psychological Bulletin*, researchers Sheldon Cohen of Carnegie-Mellon University and Thomas Ashby Wills of Cornell University Medical College reported that communicating with others who value us for our own worth and experiences counterbalances stress-caused threats to our self-esteem, and that communicating with others distracts us from worrying and helps promote positive moods. They point out, too, that we needn't suffer stress to achieve the same results.

In *The Healing Brain* authors Robert Ornstein and David Sobel, M.D., suggest that the brain's primary purpose is to guard the body against illness, and contact with other people makes the job easier.

SOCIAL ISOLATION

Some people instinctively know they feel better and accomplish more when they socialize with others. Cutting yourself off from people stul-

49

tifies the brain. And although we also need time alone to ponder and collect thoughts, when solitude is carried to extremes the mind can turn on itself. After my first winter alone when I moved to a mountain community where I didn't know anyone, friends who called said, "Your voice sounds so funny. Kind of like you're in a tunnel."

Circumstances had precluded my getting out and about after the move. Before I had unpacked my father died, and my mother, who suffers from Alzheimer's, entered a nursing facility. It took months to settle their affairs in a distant place. The long winter arrived before I was able to make friends in my new community, leaving me unprepared for the following isolation.

One long-distance friend said, "Rita, you've been alone too long. You've had no one to bounce your thoughts off of and they're bouncing off your own brain."

I had exercised my body with brisk walks and yoga, but had failed to exercise my brain with healing human interchange.

Contrast my experience with that of Carole Bryan, a management consultant and instructor who moved to a new town less than a year ago. Within a week she got a list from the local Chamber of Commerce and attended meetings on a search-and-find-friends mission; the associations she found appealing she joined. She also followed activities and events listed in the local newspaper. She says aloud what many feel but fail to act on: "Without friends I would be lonely."

In her quest to meet people, Carole took another step lauded by health experts: She checked out groups not designed solely for socialization.

Laurence Grimm, clinical psychologist and professor at the University of Illinois, Chicago, suggests getting involved with organizations geared to specific interests, rather than those serving as meeting places for lonely people. "Groups designed just for meeting people are usually attended by people frustrated to begin with," he says.

LONELINESS IS BAD FOR HEALTH

Henrik Ibsen proclaimed that the strongest man in the world is he who stands most alone. American society seems to agree with the 19th century playwright and poet by emphasizing individualism.

Yet this philosophy promotes loneliness, a universal human condition. Loneliness has been defined as an unpleasant experience, mood or feeling brought about by a discrepancy between what a person wants from relationships and the perception of what he or she gets from them.

Psychotherapist Shirley Harrison says she sees much loneliness, especially in people who are depressed and those suffering from anxiety. "I see people who are very lonely and who struggle to form relationships. They feel others are going to ask too much from them. They are distrustful. They've been burned in relationships. After the school years things become shallower. They say they enjoy spouses, children, co-workers, but don't really make friends to pal around with."

The numbers of lonely grow. One-person households have increased 173 percent in the past 13 years. Since 50 percent of our physical condition reflects the way we live, the emphasis on independence isn't all that healthy, says Milton Miller, M.D., retired psychiatry professor at the University of California at Los Angeles.

Socially isolated people are at two to three times greater risk of premature death than those involved with others, says Miller. The most important involvements are those that are ongoing and supportive, not those that simply blossom for short periods during catastrophic life events.

A person's attitudes can predict whether he or she is prone to suffering loneliness. Unfortunately, depressed and neurotic people, and those with low self-esteem and cynical outlooks, are more likely to suffer from loneliness, according to Joseph Stokes and Ira Levin, psychologists at the University of Illinois, Chicago. Levin and Stokes believe these problems relate to loneliness because they reflect a negative, pessimistic view of the self. Cynicism and rejection of others don't always reflect low self-esteem, but they may turn potential friends off.

No particular group of people, no discomfort, can cause loneliness; it comes from within.

And the notion that friends can't fill the same need as family members is false. Robert L. Rubinstein, anthropologist at the Philadelphia Geriatric Center, studied cultural variations in how never-married, childless women develop kinship-like ties with non-blood-related people. He says many cultures consider friends as close as kin because of shared experiences. "The changes in our society—fewer children, multiple marriages, longer lives, people having relatives from multiple marriages—require a rethinking of how we reckon ties."

SOCIAL SUPPORT CAN REPLACE FAMILY

Rubinstein's studies of various cultures show that social support networks *can* be more successful than traditional families. He believes we're socialized into thinking never-married older women and men form fewer successful relationships substituting friends for spouses, in-laws and children. "It's a stereotype, and not necessarily true," he says.

The problem, however, arises as we age. Those with families have a greater "moral certainty" that they'll be taken care of in American culture. Blood relatives, more often than friends, help care for the elderly. Friendship is individually negotiated; it's not morally obligatory unless a personal bonding similar to kinship takes place.

DISTRESS CAUSED BY LACK OF SOCIAL SUPPORT

Joseph Becker, Ph.D., a professor in the Department of Psychiatry and Behavioral Sciences, University of Washington, Seattle, says research literature doesn't give adequate attention to distress, particularly when a person expects help. "What we expect depends on our social background. People in the main cultural stream expect support. If it's not forthcoming, the void is very hurtful."

Lacking supportive social relationships—especially with close, confiding friends—can cause loneliness. Simultaneously, depressives often dump too much on friends," says Becker. "They go into a friendship with unrealistic expectations, become dependent and overly concerned about what they get from the relationship. They tend to be less sensitive in reciprocal aspects of the friendship."

A person can inherit a predisposition to depression, in which case lack of support networks may not be a factor. Depression can also reflect one's excessively high standards for him- or herself. The person believes "If I were perfect enough, I would be loved," says Becker. "Perfection isn't necessary in friendships. But we do need awareness that developing a friendship involves costs, as well as benefits."

Those costs include spending time and effort as well as tolerating broken promises, irritability, attached strings, mood changes, and a host of other human traits that we *also* bring into relationships. The alternative to paying the price, however, can be loneliness.

VOLUNTEERISM

Millions of people find that volunteer work serves their friendship needs, and one of America's greatest natural resources is its volunteers. Like a golden mother lode, the vein gets richer and the returns greater as time passes—for both giver and receiver.

Ruth Dever, an 80-year-old volunteer with the literacy program in Colton, California, lives on a small fixed income. She says her work with a formerly unemployed truck driver who has learned to read and write under her tutelage helps keep her young and feeling good.

Dever counts herself among those volunteers who get pleasure from helping others. But they also help themselves more than they realize; such altruistic behavior promotes good physical and mental health, according to medical professionals.

Doctors and social scientists attending a 1989 conference at the Institute for the Advancement of Health in New York advanced the theory that altruistic behavior might enhance health because it reduces helpless and depressive feelings. They suggest that helping others both reduces feelings of loneliness and produces social connectedness.

Most people involved in volunteer work aren't aware of the good they're doing for themselves; the effort simply makes them feel good.

So desirable and respected is this ''feel-good'' sense that nearly 50 percent of adult Americans volunteer their time manning crisis hotlines, working with the homeless, the illiterate and/or the abused, raising funds for everything from cancer research to saving whales. Time given to volunteerism increased 35 percent in the past five years.

Although it's unlikely people volunteer because they're aware it promotes good health, volunteering grew from one in six persons in 1965 to one in four in 1975. It has continued to increase every year since. Researchers attribute the rise in part to Baby Boomers approaching middle age. Traditionally, young adults ages 18 to 24 are least likely to do volunteer work, while those ages 35 to 50 are most apt to donate their time.

Volunteering doesn't require wealth or extra time. Working women donate more hours than homemakers. And America's volunteers cut swaths across all socioeconomic lines. According to a 1989 Gallup Poll, nearly a quarter of volunteers come from families with annual incomes under $20,000.

VOLUNTEERISM BOOSTS HEALTH

The late Hans Selye, founder of modern stress research, believed the affection and gratitude one received from others for doing good helped protect the doer from life's stresses.

Some researchers believe warm feelings we get from altruistic acts affect endorphins, the brain's natural "feel-good" opiates. Endorphins, amino acids produced by the pituitary gland to reduce pain through the nervous system, also cause the phenomena known as runner's high and the exalted feelings experienced through deep meditation. Further research indicates the good feelings triggered by endorphins may boost the immune system.

The release of certain hormones that contribute to good health takes place when humans interact with one another, says sociologist Karl Landis of the University of Michigan, Ann Arbor.

Volunteering also provides a sense of control over one's life through the freedom of choice it involves. People with choices about life events and those with greater capacities for friendship rate higher on well-being scales, says Landis.

GROWTH IN VOLUNTEERISM

With the upswing in volunteerism comes an increase of more than 30 percent in students choosing fields such as social work. "Not only are they motivated to this type of work by media focus on social problems facing the country, but many are touched by drugs or alcohol dependence, AIDS and/or aging within their families. The issues are hitting home," says Ione Vargus, dean of Temple University's School of Social Administration in Philadelphia.

Professor Morley Glicken, director of the Department of Social Work at California State University, San Bernardino, says, "Not only are the young experiencing a resurgence of altruism, but many older people who chose status- and money-oriented careers are now realizing their work didn't lead to satisfaction in their lives. So those who 20 years ago would have perferred social work but didn't go that route are making changes," says Glicken.

HOW WE BECOME ALTRUISTIC

Professionals studying altruism also find that young children who seem concerned about others' welfare often come from families with a history of unselfishness. Researchers and child-behavior specialists who study hereditary patterns believe that not only do altruistic families foster benevolence by serving as role models, but that they also pass on genes that make their offspring more likely to become givers.

Studies at the University of London Institute of Psychiatry showed selfless children tended to become even more empathic and nurturing as they aged. They also tended to mimic the more altruistic parent rather than the more selfish one, according to David W. Fulker, who took part in the London Institute studies and is now at the Institute for Behavioral Genetics at the University of Colorado.

Altruistic individuals tend to select similar people as both friends and marriage partners.

Children who don't inherit a propensity toward altruism, however, can learn charitable qualities; so says Nell Noddings, a Stanford University education professor. She believes it's possible to help teach children more caring attitudes through our school systems.

Noddings says many schools are sending students out to nursing homes, hospitals, and other helping institutions to learn firsthand about the needs—which is better than sitting in a classroom and learning about them abstractly.

Samuel P. Oliner and Pearl M. Oliner, authors of *The Altruistic Personality: Rescuers of Jews in Nazi Europe*, write that schools need to become institutions that not only prepare students for academic achievement but also help them learn to care about others.

MEETING THE NEEDS OF VOLUNTEERS

Another group interested in the growth of altruism is marketing researchers, who conduct separate studies because they want to teach nonprofit agencies about tapping into such valuable resources.

Research at the University of Wisconsin-La Crosse, for example, centers on volunteers' personalities. The La Crosse research, conducted by marketing researchers in the Business Administration Department, found volunteers want much more affection from others than typical individuals and they get it from volunteer work.

By catering to this need for love and esteem, agencies needing volunteers can learn some necessary lessons about recruiting and keeping their volunteers. Irene M. Thorelli, a La Crosse researcher, says knowing how to enlist and retain good volunteers is vital if our nation wants to keep its helping institutions flourishing.

The La Crosse studies show that volunteers get their desired extra affection and a conduit for expressing love from volunteer work—because often their paying jobs, and sometimes their home lives, don't satisfy those needs.

The La Crosse studies show volunteers need direct contact with those they serve, and expect a return on their investment. As a volunteer, if you don't get positive feedback for your efforts, find another organization to give your time to—and don't feel guilty about leaving one that's not meeting your needs.

With increasing populations, urbanization and its attendant alienation, the need for volunteers will continue to grow.

Volunteering is negative only if you develop unrealistic self-expectations, or expect too much from the people for whom you're working. It's a generous gift, presented without thought of remuneration, yet it yields great rewards for the giver because it becomes a form of friendship.

HOW TO GET INFORMATION ABOUT LOCAL VOLUNTEER ORGANIZATIONS

Call or write:

AIDS hotline (for information or to volunteer assistance to AIDS victims), 800–342–AIDS (English); 800–344–SIDA (**en Español**).

American Cancer Society, 1599 Clifton Rd NE, Atlanta, GA 30329.

American Friends Service Committee, 1501 Cherry St, Philadelphia, PA 19102.

Foster Grandparents Program, 1100 Vermont Ave NW, Ste 6100 Washington, DC 20525.

Habitat for Humanity, Habitat and Church Street, Americus, GA 31709.

The Holiday Project, Department NW, Box 6829, FDR Station, New York, NY 10150–1906.

Literacy Volunteers of America, 5795 Widewaters Parkway, Syracuse, NY 13214.

Mothers Against Drunk Drivers (MADD), PO Box 541688, Dallas, TX 75354–1688.

National Braille Association, 1290 University Ave, Rochester, NY 14607.

Prison Fellowship Ministries, PO Box 17500, Washington, DC 20041–0500.

Salvation Army, 799 Bloomfield Ave, Verona, NJ 07044.

For location of a nearby volunteer center, The National Center, 1111 N 19th St, Ste 500, Arlington, VA 22209; 703–276–0542.

LEISURE TIME BEGETS FRIENDS

A Japanese man with four cameras strung around his neck and five children following him struggled up a hill in Yellowstone National Park just ahead of me. You couldn't miss the scowl on his face when he turned around periodically to check on his small charges. He looked over their heads and said, "If I have to look at another geyser, I'm going to throw up."

I agreed. At first seeing dozens of geysers with their bubbling, spouting pools surrounded by colorful crusted chemicals proved exhilarating. Then it became wearisome.

Later, sitting upstairs in the lodge with my feet resting on a rail as I watched the activity in the main room below, I was joined by several people who started telling all sorts of lively stories. Chatting with strangers turned out to be the most enjoyable part of the day. It was pure leisure in our madcap world of harried lives with never enough time to take pleasure in doing just *nothing*. Health experts say we're so out of touch with real "leisure" we don't know how to use or enjoy it when we get it.

These same experts say we fumble at the slack in our lives caused by technology, fewer children, smaller living spaces to care for, and shortened workweeks. How can we dispute noted psychologist and philosopher B. F. Skinner, who said, "Once satiated and free from aversive stimulation, man, like many other species, becomes inactive and goes to sleep."

LACK OF LEISURE

The 19th century English novelist George Eliot had another view: "Leisure is gone; gone where the spinning-wheels are gone, and the pack horses, and the slow wagons, and the peddlers who brought bargains to the door on sunny afternoons."

We feel this lack of leisure and attendant pleasure down to our bones. Yet the Puritan ethic in us—that need to accomplish something every moment—prevents our feeling at peace with pure downtime.

Some health professionals believe we're so lacking in knowledge of what to do with free time it may require training to set us on the right track.

Until ten or 15 years ago, we defined leisure almost by default. "Whatever time was left over after working, cooking, taking care of the children, managing a household, was considered leisure," says Howard E. Tinsley, psychology professor at Southern Illinois University at Carbondale.

Leisure, unlike other researched areas of our lives, hasn't come under much scrutiny. Yet the professionals say people who know how to enjoy leisure have more positive outlooks on life and acquire more friends, and that couples who engage in recreational activities together are happier and enjoy stronger marriages.

FINDING LEISURE

So where does that leave us? Health professionals say it's good for us, yet we can't go out and buy leisure like we can no-fat salad dressing.

Clearly, leisure's definition has changed. Tinsley defines it as:

1. Freedom of choice
2. Intrinsic motivation
3. A sense of stimulation
4. The need to commit or invest

Elaborating, Tinsley says, "Freedom of choice means a person must choose without force. Intrinsic motivation shows the pure pleasure one derives from the activity. The sense of stimulation needs to include optimal arousal, but not too much or one is likely to feel overloaded. A sense of commitment means an investment of some sort.

"On the other hand, I read an article about a runner who said you have to do it when you don't feel like it—day after day. He's really losing the sense that he's choosing to do this. When you get up feeling you don't really want to run today but you have to, you've created a second job instead of a leisure activity."

Workaholics may experience leisure on the job if they find their work so engrossing and pleasurable that it's a preferred choice. Other leisure activities can evolve from a sense of novelty or arousal; but when fun disappears, so should the activity.

Leisure activity needs to fit the individual. "People are different in their approach to things. Some find it difficult to coordinate with others; they possess a strong sense of individuality. Others have a strong sense of camaraderie and need to seek out socially oriented activities. Those who rate high in independence need to take their leisure more separately," says Tinsley.

Having problems with leisure can mean unhappiness in other areas of life as well, he contends.

It's critical to find out what makes an individual feel good. When someone says, "You need to learn to meditate," or "Why don't you take up tennis?" or "A cruise would do you a world of good," or "You need more friends," he or she might be on the wrong track altogether.

Noted oncologist Carl Simonton, pioneer in the field of developing a more playful life, especially when faced with a life-threatening illness, says you can kill yourself with anything. "I can go out and kill myself on the tennis court. You can meditate yourself to death. We need to develop our own melody—our own area that we can get joy and pleasure from," he says.

If an activity is enjoyable to you personally, if you look forward to doing it again, if you set time aside just for it, if it tickles your sense of pleasure: It's probably real leisure.

MAKING TIME FOR LEISURE

A young high school art teacher, suffering stress, went on a weeklong retreat and told me she spent four days observing the goings on of an ant hill. "It was wonderful. I'm totally refreshed and relaxed." She also made some new friends at the retreat, and acknowledges that meeting them was part of the cure for her stress and burnout.

Sometimes we bemoan our shortcomings in not spending enough time with friends. Our world seems in tune with the 1980s movie *Koyaanisqatsi* (Life in Chaos) that begins with panoramic sweeps of the landscape and ends with the frenzy of a New York rush hour. The film upsets some who view it. Nerves become jangled. Yet the popular music of today's youth has the same frantic intensity, reflecting the world the young are inheriting. We long to stand on the road in idle conversation with the peddler. Making time to spend with friends nearly becomes a form of leisure itself. When we do it, however, it adds to life's richness.

PETS AS FRIENDS ARE GOOD MEDICINE

Pets don't replace human friends, but they can be a pretty close second best. Some people even consider them easier to get along with than humans.

Those who eschew people and turn to pets often have problems getting along with other humans. So be it: Pets provide surprising benefits. When we give a cat or dog a fond pat on the head, it not only gives us a lift, but research shows it gives our health a boost too. The same can be said when we care for, watch and/or listen to pet birds or fish.

The link between people and animals is as old as human life, with proof of pet dogs around the campfires of our prehistoric forebears. Perhaps a dog's antics relieved stress in the harsh lives of those long-ago people. Perhaps our ancestors knew instinctively what scientists are discovering today—that pets can enrich nearly every area of our lives.

Children, too, seem to know instinctively that pets make humans feel good—partly because old Scamp wags his tail and licks the child's face without telling him or her to wash up, dress up, or shut up.

HOW PETS AFFECT US

Pets not only accept us, but nurture and heal us as well. When we talk to pets, our blood pressure goes down; when we talk to humans, it goes up. This because talking to dogs, cats, birds, even fish is much less stressful than talking to people, according to Aaron Katcher, associate professor of psychiatry at the University of Pennsylvania's Center for the Interaction of Animals and Society.

"It's a touch-talk dialogue. When you're touching a pet it's an affectionate dialogue," he says, adding that more than 80 percent of pet owners say they talk to their charges as if they were human. Some even tell their animals personal secrets.

Pets also serve as surrogate children, so adults usually speak to them in softer, slower tones. This gentles our system—a condition good for overall health.

Katcher was among the first researchers to pinpoint the relationship among people, pets and health. By 1978, when he was a graduate student, his research indicated that people who suffer heart attacks have better survival rates the first year after an attack if they own a pet.

C. Edward Koop, former Surgeon General of the United States, said pets sometimes enhance the mental and physical welfare of disabled persons as no medicine or doctor can.

This proves true at Green Chimneys School for Disturbed Children in Brewster, New York, home to many abused and neglected children who receive "animal therapy" at the school. Children from six to 14, mostly inner-city kids from New York and surrounding cities, become permanent residents for up to three years, with part of their curriculum a "therapeutic farm."

The farm's programs include horseback riding that teaches physically or emotionally disturbed children balance as well as how to care for, groom and ride a horse. Another program teaches youngsters how to care for farm animals; they learn to handle grooming and feeding chores, and about life cycles and gestation periods. A third program teaches disabled children to nurse injured and disabled wild animals toward returning them to the wild after healing—not unlike the school's goal for children.

"The programs give kids a chance to succeed. The children learn to bond with the animals, to provide service, and to nurture—

something they may not have learned at home. It gives them a chance to love something. We get birds with wings amputated in a shooting, and the kids see these birds still have a remarkable will to survive. They learn they too can survive with handicaps," says Paul Kupchok, farm director at the school.

PET THERAPY

Pet therapy isn't just for children. Nursing-home residents perk up when they are visited by pet organizations bearing furry creatures.

In the past few years institutions have lightened up, allowing pets into their facilities once it became overwhelmingly evident that pet-assisted therapy works miracles for the elderly.

When I took my collie to visit my mother in the nursing facility, Mom's first reaction was to fetch the thirsty dog a pail of water. I could tell by my mother's smile and actions that she loved helping the dog, who lapped water up as if he hadn't had a drink in three days. She began talking about cats she'd had to other patients sitting on the patio enjoying the sun. And they in turn told about pets they had cared for. The wheelchair-bound patients could hardly wait to run their hands through my dog's shaggy fur and talk soothingly into his ear.

Research shows animals make people in nursing homes feel good because they conjure up happy memories; they help the patients feel in control of their lives; they offer an opportunity to show affection; and they renew the patients' link to nature, since many elderly people grew up on farms. They also transport those who are bedridden, for a time, on a make-believe trip outside the facility's confines.

Therapist-physiologist Elizabeth Corson of Columbus, Ohio, and her husband, Samuel Corson, M.D., are noted experts on human and pet interactions who say cats, in particular, give many older people reasons for living. And when people feel down, taking care of an animal makes them feel strong and nurturing. "They can feel on top of things," they say.

The good feeling animals can impart also finds its way into prison systems that now allow inmates to keep small pets. The programs help build self-confidence and self-esteem.

Corson agrees with Katcher about pets being good for people, because "they accept people with all their flaws. We don't do that with other people."

Katcher adds, "It's impossible to get negative, verbal feedback from dogs. They don't evaluate us. An animal can't tell us we're stupid. It can't say cruel things."

A pet also serves as a source of pride and helps build self-esteem. When we groom a cat or dog, we can anticipate praise for making it look good.

We interact with fish and birds in a slightly different manner, but they are no less effective.

Tina Ellenbogen, representing the Delta Society, a nonprofit international resource center on human-animal interactions, says 52 percent of households in the United States own a cat or a dog, and 14 percent own both. In addition, fish ownership has reached an all-time high, and bird ownership has also increased, possibly because these pets require much less room and lower expenditures for food and upkeep.

The American Veterinary Medical Association reports that bird owners tend to be renters living in large cities, while cat and dog owners often live outside metropolitan areas.

As for fish: "Watching them in a tank is a very effective way to relax," says Katcher. Indeed, tests conducted at the center in Pennsylvania show that watching fish can lower a hypertensive's blood pressure. Other studies show that contemplating a fish tank lowers anxiety much as hypnosis does before dental surgery.

Bird-watching can do much the same, except that two different types of bird interaction exist. Birds such as finches become like feathered fish—they're for watching and not interacting with. On the other hand, birds such as parrots, cockatiels and macaws do involve interaction. "They groom you and you groom them. They take food from you mouth. They talk to you, so they are more like cats and dogs," says Katcher.

Pets specialists also speculate that a pet's antics, especially those that make us laugh, boost our health by distracting us from stressful situations. Laughter also appears to boost the immune system.

PETS HELP RELIEVE DEPRESSION

Depression responds well to pet therapy. In the late 1960s the Corsons took playful dogs to a psychiatric hospital at Ohio State University and worked with depressed patients who hadn't responded to traditional treatment. When some patients responded to the "pet-therapy," other treatment centers began using their methods.

Yet Corson warns that research indicating longer lives for people who own pets might be misleading. "It could be that people who choose to live with and take care of pets have the types of personalities that help them live longer.

"In some cases pets aren't good for people—if the owner has allergies, if the pet is troublesome, or if it causes problems between family members. But under the right circumstances, pets are definitely healthful," she says.

Whether we own a bird, dog, cat, fish, or other pet; and whether the setting is our own home, a nursing home, a hospital or prison: Most of us are richer for lessons the beloved animal teaches us about caring and unconditional love—which itself might lead to longer and more healthful lives.

5 WHAT MAKES A FRIENDSHIP ZING?

... and what attracts us in the first place?

Society may change, but the individual's need for close personal relationships will endure. Humans will always require the companionship of other humans.

We have just gone through what many called the "Me" generation. It was a time of striving for material goods, and psychologist Melvyn Kinder writes in *Going Nowhere Fast* that the most obvious casualties of the ambition treadmill are family and friends.

On a lighter note, Alhleigh Brilliant, Ph.D., of the University of California at Berkeley writes in *I Feel Much Better, Now That I've Given up Hope*, "I've accumulated enough to be the envy of all my friends, if I had any friends."

FROM "ME" TO "WE"

Marriage and family counselor Dennis L. Harris, director of the Living, Learning and Relating Foundation in Ontario, California, agrees that Americans are searching for deeper meanings to their lives following the "Me" decades of the 1960s and '70s. "The breakdown of families and the drive toward affluence, wealth and power have been left wanting," he says. "The 'We' generation is emerging."

To get in touch with our need for friendships, sharing and community—to change from "Me" to "We"—Harris recommends that we:

69

• Develop a sense of immediacy. Most people who go into counseling are dealing with a sense of brokenness or lack of meaning in their lives. They need to take positive action on those feelings immediately, because it will translate to power over the situation.

• Realize that we only find out about ourselves through relationships. We need other people to help us figure out who and what we are. We can't do it in a mirror.

• Give without expectation of a reward. We should strive to give more than we get back. Usually, then, we receive more than anticipated.

THE NEED FOR FRIENDS IS UNIVERSAL

The profundity of friendship exhibits itself daily. The *Orange County Register*, a widely circulated Southern California newspaper, runs one column about friendships and another chronicling stories of best friends. It also assigns a "mall beat" reporter to cover happenings at shopping malls where people gather as they once did in the town square or local grocery store.

Wherever we meet, however, we're attracted more to some people than others, and it is they who become our special friends. Why?

THE FILTERING SYSTEM

Sociologists and psychologists use the term "filtering" when talking about the early stages of friendship. We begin with an infinite population of potential friends and end with a select group. What happens during the filtering process?

Research shows we're initially drawn to others, whether consciously or unconsciously, because of their attractiveness, race, sex and age.

John D. Edwards, associate professor of psychology at Loyola University, Chicago, tells us how we filter friendships and proceed to deepen them.

• Filtering usually begins with proximity, bringing into play the arbitrary factors that bring people into contact with each other and determine whether they will become friends or enemies. "In general, people who are in close proximity to us seem to present the first stage."

• Next comes physical appearance. "We think it would be less important in friendship than in romance, but lo and behold, we initially attract friends through similarities in physical characteristics. We're aware of race, gender and age. Social status, too, comes into play."

Research by sociologist Debra Umberson at the University of Texas at Austin supports the theory that attractive people might have a greater choice of friends because of the response they elicit. "Teachers in early school years pay more attention to attractive children. If you're arrested, you're more likely to get better treatment if you're attractive, unless you're charged with embezzlement," says Umberson. "People just respond far more favorably to attractive people."

Attractive people are afforded more opportunities to perform, and receive more positive evaluations from others, according to Umberson. "They're also examined less carefully for defective performances," she adds. Attractive people experience less stress in their lives because others treat them more positively and they are thus presented with fewer problems in daily interactions, according to her studies.

Further, they develop more self-confidence—which, in turn, increases popularity even more. "Clearly we know people who are just charming regardless of the way they look, but attractiveness helps," says Umberson.

As the cliché contends, "Birds of a feather flock together," according to Edwards. "Those who don't fit the norm—who are excessively fat or short, for example—have more difficulty than those who do. The physical self elicits response and often becomes the basis for groups people join." Thus tall people, or people of a particular ethnic background, might gather more readily than people with very different physical appearances.

• After physical likeness we look for other similarities, such as beliefs and interests. "We have another cliché about opposites attracting, but research supports the complementary," Edwards says. "There are exceptions, of course. Sometimes friends agree on differences and one person is dominant and the other submissive. In some respects these people are opposites but they are different in a complementary fashion. They simply agree to fulfill each other's needs."

• The first three filters lead to another that is based on reinforcement. "We tend to like things associated with pleasant outcomes. So more research says we are attracted to people who praise and compliment us," says Edwards. But "We don't find these things out until we have gotten to know another person a little bit"; thus people who meet under pleasant circumstances stand a better chance of becoming permanent friends than those who meet under adverse conditions. Reinforcement needs a framework, so while we filter reinforcement, we share mutually satisfying activities such as sports, ecology or the arts. "If people enjoy activities together, it helps cement the relationship," says Edwards. At this point, the potential for maintaining or dissolving the friendship becomes greatest, and we move to the next filtering step.

- "The level of intimacy between people hinges on the reciprocity rule," Edwards says. "If they share on an equal footing, the number of things they are willing to talk about gradually increases. If, on the other hand, one person remains relatively cool and the other is looking for a deeper relationship, the friendship won't go anywhere."

When people go through these filters successfully their friendship can last a lifetime even if they wind up a continent apart: Shared memories and interest in each other's current activities take over and help keep the relationship vibrant.

CHARISMA

There are many exceptions to the filtering theory. We all know people who attract others like flowers attract bees. Psychologists liken this situation to economics: "A person who is selectively, yet not all that readily, available, is more attractive than someone who is always there. The rarer something is, the more value we place on it—unless it seems completely unattainable," says Edwards. "People who are charismatic have a tendency to make others feel special, and that adds to their attractiveness."

When rarity and charisma combine, we enjoy being a part of the result. Edwards cautions, however, that "rarity" doesn't mean unavailability or snobbishness. Most charismatic people truly like being around others, and others in turn feel good in their company. They usually have gregarious, open, fluid personalities. Interesting in their own right, they share intimacies; but they also like to *listen*.

At the opposite end of the spectrum sits the hermit, who doesn't care if he or she attracts people or not.

"Most of us are in the middle of the range," says Edwards.

BIRDS-OF-A-FEATHER TYPES AND PROTEIN PEOPLE

Our place on the need-for-people scale depends on both our genetic inheritance and our childhood environment. A person who is open and gregarious usually had at least one parent with the same disposition. Yet if someone is gregarious by nature but doesn't have the personality to go with it, problems surface, according to Edwards. "People on the high-need scale who don't have friendship skills become lonely and depressed."

Another difference among people when it comes to friends involves "cognitive complexity." Some people are uncomfortable unless they are around people who look, act and think as they do. They allow little diversity in their approach to selecting friends, preferring people who don't disturb their political, religious or social beliefs.

In the opposite corner we find the "protein personality," the person who can stretch or shrink to accommodate a wide range of friends from different age, ethnic and socioeconomic groups. "These people can see beyond the filters discussed earlier," says Edwards. "They look at *individuals*. They seek profound qualities more than superficial ones. The cognitive complexity of protein personalities allows them to enjoy variety. People who allow little complexity are uncomfortable around them because cognitively simple people evaluate in only one dimension. They see the world in black and white."

Protein people possess a "we" mentality. They move quickly through the filtering system.

MAKING BEST FRIENDS

Once through the filtering system, we're ready to proceed toward those few people who become our close friends; whose intimate friendships provide the zing that makes our lives richer. The relationships allow us to be ourselves and let our hair down.

Research suggests that people high in intimacy-motivation react more harmoniously in groups, and they smile more. Yet men and women absorb different values when they open to intimacy. Psychologist Fred B. Bryant of Loyola University in Chicago says high intimacy-motivation in women produces greater happiness and gratification. In men, it links with lack of strain and lack of uncertainty.

Whatever the motivation, however, intimacy doesn't mean dumping problems on a friend. Rather it means sharing ourselves— our hopes, dreams and day-to-day feelings.

Studies of women who manage to excel in business despite great obstacles show them rich in friendships and support systems. They rarely unload their troubles on friends, according to psychologist Martin Barry Schlosser of Clarity Consulting Corp. in Westport, Connecticut. They confide problems occasionally, but more often search for solutions.

Developing close friendships is also likened to a feeling of coming home.

COMING HOME

M. Scott Peck, M.D., writes in *The Different Drum* that after terrible years at a boarding school where rugged individualism was extolled and being part of the "in" crowd was a virtue, he found peace and a coming home at a small Quaker school where there was a sense of community.

I experienced this once when I walked into a restaurant in a strange town. It turned out it was a gathering place for many locals because its owner, with whom I later developed a close friendship, created a communal atmosphere. "I never hired anyone who didn't smile," says Barbara Cunningham. "Good food draws customers initially; genuinely liking your customers keeps them coming back."

The restaurant's patrons seemed a diversified lot—young and old, businesspeople and clerks, men and women. Yet the setting made you feel they were all your friends. There was a sense of community, of comfort, of coming home.

The same thing can happen at a one-on-one level. Bette Ross says, "There is something about friendship beyond likes and dislikes and getting along; there is a feeling of being drawn, a magnetizing, that can happen almost before you know the person. It's happened two or three time to me with women who were in my life so briefly we never had a chance to explore what it was that attracted us to each other. People meet on vacation or at a weekend conference. You know you could be friends."

"It's magic that draws people together," says Stormy Sandquist of New Mexico. "You can't make people like you. But if you are interested in them and open to friendship, it can happen."

Whether we call it magic, a coming home, filtering, or instinctive behavior, more is at work with friendships than we suspect.

In *Man's Search for Meaning*, psychiatrist Viktor E. Frankl, who survived the Nazi concentration camps and wrote of how man can transcend suffering and find meaning to life, says we can do this "by experiencing another human being in his very uniqueness—by loving him."

FAMILY MEMBERS AS BEST FRIENDS

We love our immediate and extended families, but they are seldom our best friends. A few people interviewed said spouses, siblings or children were among their best friends, and one named her father. But relatives often provide a different sort of relationship.

"I talk about different things with my friends than I do with family," says one man. "My children (now grown) tend to be quite conservative, and I'm very liberal, so when we're together we avoid subjects like politics, religion and philosophy. I really enjoy discussing those subjects with my friends because they think more like I do."

"We used to have terrible arguments about politics," says a woman. "My sister went along with what her husband said. During the Civil Rights Movement and Vietnam conflict, it was difficult for me to be around them because I couldn't really be myself. Eventually I learned to keep silent about certain subjects and enjoy my sister and brother-in-law for who and what they were. And as we got older, I realized there were other things we *could* talk about. They are more dear to me now."

Being more intimate with friends than with family is a somewhat new phenomenon, according to Gordon Clanton, sociology professor at San Diego State University. Before World War II we didn't refer to family members as "best friends," yet they filled many roles best friends fill today. We had best friends, but we didn't count on them for support as we do today; we called on our families for that. Best friends often lived near one another all their lives. Because of today's greatly increased mobility—a majority of people move at least five times—lifelong best-friend relationships have become rare.

THE MEANINGS OF "BEST FRIENDS" AND "FAMILY" HAVE CHANGED

"My sense is that having a family member as a best friend is a modern phenomenon," says Clanton. "Our grandparents never used that language. The idea of a family member as a best friend came along after World War II. Previously, most of us had stronger family ties. We counted on our families for help. People lived in one place a long time and grew up with close blood ties. We had family and we had best friends; there was a clear distinction.

"After World War II we became more mobile; peers became more important, parents less. Peers became our best friends. They reinforced the different values we were developing. And the family took a beating because we didn't stay in the small towns and neighborhoods of our childhoods. We couldn't rely on families for help because we didn't live near them."

Although the idea of best friends as replacements for family support systems seems a good one, lifelong friendships are actually rarer than they were before Americans hit the road. Some people refer to their friends as being "like family," but neither family nor friends play the parts they once did. When we say best friends are more important than family, therefore, it's because of the erosion of family relationships.

Few generational gaps existed before World War II. "A generation gap as a national problem wasn't evident until the 1950s," says Clanton. "Then people began to develop stronger bonds with those who thought as they did. Sociology was developed for chronicling the pluses and minuses of communities. Most of us wouldn't want a return to a time when the entire community knew our business. We wouldn't want the church knocking on our doors telling us we had been remiss in church attendance. So we shouldn't romanticize the village concept of our forebears."

SOURCES OF SUPPORT ARE UNPREDICTABLE

Nor should we romanticize today's best-friend concept. Language people use describing their friendships reflects how we're organized. "A whole lot of what people say when talking about family, friends or neighbors shows that these sources of support aren't as predictable and secure as they once were," says Clanton.

Insecurity in social support is catching up with us, and more people than ever need lasting, supportive, enriching friendships.

Without realizing it, we may be searching for replacements for the family and lifelong friends of the past—or for a romanticized version of them.

HUSBANDS AND WIVES AS BEST FRIENDS

There is not always friendship between husbands and wives. But when it *is* there, it may be the glue for a successful marriage.

More men than women report that their spouses are their best friends. Phillip Zimbardo, director of the Stanford Shyness Clinic, says men are more likely to identify wives as best friends because they don't tend to make intimate friends outside marriage, whereas women do.

During an interview for *Entrepreneurial Woman* magazine on whether it's easier owning a business if a person is married or single, Sharon Miller of Midland, Michigan, said it was easier being single—but she would prefer marriage again. However, "It's kind of tough finding the right man," she said. "It would have to be someone who would share friendship, respect and love—in that order. If I can't have friendship, love won't get me very far. And I must have respect to have friendship."

Some thoughts of people who say their spouses or "significant others" are among their best friends:

- "My partner is one of my best friends; we share very personal experiences."—Karen Olden.
- "A ten."—Sharlya Gold of her husband.
- "He was the greatest friend I'll ever have or love."—Marion Lapins, 75, of her late husband.
- "Tom is terrific. Incredibly supportive, loving, understanding, trustworthy, funny and gentle. I can tell him anything."—Paula Emik.

- ''The very best.''—Richard Teeling.
- ''All other friendships aside, my husband is the best friend I shall ever have. No other friendship could undergo the stress and strain of our marriage.''—Mary Swaney.
- ''We could not be closer or more concerned for each other's welfare and comfort than we have been for nearly 56 years. We have very close communication, respect each other's opinions and desires. Our friendship and love are A-1!''—An 81-year-old man who didn't want his name used.
- ''He was tops. After four years, I still miss him terribly.'' —Lucile Irving, 89, of her late husband.
- ''Great. We couldn't have had 42 years of marriage unless we were good friends.''—A 64-year-old man who didn't want his name used.

The quality of friendship is best determined by how good we feel when we're around a person—be it a spouse, family member or someone we've just met at a party. We may initially use the filtering system, but through it we find those who make us feel as if we have come home. Those are the friendships that zing.

Home is the resort of love, of joy, of peace, and plenty, where supporting and supported, polished friends and dearest relatives mingle into bliss.
　　　　　　　—James Thomson, 18th century Scottish poet

6 THE SHY STRANGER

... or why am I telling you these things?

STRANGERS AS CONFIDANTS

I was eating breakfast in a Las Vegas coffee shop when a weary gambler sat down at the counter beside me and began telling me about his run of bad luck the previous night. He proceeded to tell me he gambled for a living, that he had once been a computer programmer for a large company, how his marriage had dissolved, and how he felt about his father. He revealed feelings about parts of his life we often don't even share with best friends.

Opening up to a stranger, however, isn't uncommon. "Most of us are less shy with strangers than with people we know," says Phillip Zimbardo, director of the Stanford Shyness Clinic.

"It's like personal disclosures to a bartender or a hairdresser. Some people feel more comfortable confessing to a stranger when they primarily want to get something off their chests and get some generalized sympathy. It's probably not consciously done, but it's a catharsis. And they don't have to face the stranger on Monday morning."

For many people, intense, revealing encounters occur on weekends away from normal work and home routines. The more leisurely setting relieves a person of everyday constraints and the disclosure seems safe because the listener isn't evaluating the speaker.

"Strangers don't know your friends, so you're safe there too; they can't reveal your inadequacies," says Zimbardo.

With best friends, on the other hand, we might feel uneasy sharing personal vulnerabilities. We might even be a little afraid they will tell mutual friends what we have told them in confidence.

Sharing with strangers is especially important to men, many of whom lack best friends.

"There are many more strangers than best friends," says Zimbardo. "And best friends aren't alway around; strangers are. We can always talk to a cab driver or a barber, or pay a therapist to listen to us," he says, adding that studies of prostitutes in San Francisco showed that a surprising number of clients paid them to listen to their secrets. "Prostitutes said many of their clients were shy, married men who wanted to talk about their sexual needs more than they wanted to engage in sex. They wanted to talk about things they couldn't share with their wives."

Since it's healthier to disclose to others than to keep everything bottled up, Zimbardo sees nothing wrong with revealing secrets to strangers. Yet there are drawbacks: "A friend can give you advice, and disclosing to a friend strengthens a relationship," he says. Further, talking to strangers doesn't help solve a problem. It may even let a shy person avoid seeking a solution.

OVERCOMING SHYNESS

Shyness itself can be a problem when it comes to developing friendships, although once a shy person makes a friend, he or she often proves to be the most loyal companion of all.

Consider these statements from people who acknowledge their reticence:

- "I struggle with it, yet I cherish my alone times and am not always willing to have them invaded."

- Another says, "I tend to wait for the other person to make the first approach. It's hard for me to talk to strangers."
- A soft-spoken man says, "It's hard finding people who would want to be my friend or with whom I would want to be friends. I'm shy and generally quiet."
- A librarian says, "To make a real friend means having to offer someone else the same qualities I value. I'm reluctant to give that much to most of the people I meet. I usually choose not to pursue a friendship because I'm shy about taking the initiative."
- Another person says, "It's difficult for me to make friends because I can be very bashful and just sit and not speak to or interact with people."

Research shows shyness affects about 15 percent of the population, and it's an inherited tendency in about 40 percent of us. Some of it stems from fear of rejection because the person is not as well educated or attractive, or because he or she has a handicap—a stutter, for example.

Environment also affects shy people from childhood on. "Some kids come into the world with a predisposition to shyness, but their environment can have an impact on its development." So says Laura Kamptner, professor of psychology at California State University, San Bernardino. "If a child has reserved parents, chances are they don't provide experiences that help overcome the child's reticence. The parents don't have many friends over, so the child gets a double dose: genetics and environment. If parents are concerned, they need to change themselves. They need to look at their own behavior and the kinds of messages they convey to their children. If parents are uncomfortable around company, the child learns people are anxiety-provoking."

SHYNESS CAN BE BENEFICIAL

I remember the girl in my Brownie Troop whose mother asked timidly if her daughter was making friends: "She's shy, you know."

Yes, she was making friends. I watched her approach people and softly ask, "Would you like to buy some Girl Scout cookies?" Could they resist the dark eyes that looked down after she asked? "Oh, thank you," she'd say when they said yes. "Would you like to buy two boxes?" The eyes rose again at just the right moment. They always bought two—or more.

Shyness can be positive in another way. "A shy person is more sensitive to other people. He or she pays attention in a way others do not," says David Rowe, behavioral geneticist and psychology professor at the University of Arizona.

It may also serve to protect others on occasion. "Shyness possibly makes people a little more reticent to take action in some situations where the action might be detrimental to society," says Kamptner.

THE NEGATIVE SIDE OF SHYNESS

People sometimes use their shyness to take advantage of other people, according to Los Angeles psychologist Gary Emery, author of *Positive Force*. They'll ask a friend to return damaged merchandise or make airline reservations for them with the excuse that they're uncomfortable about it.

At one time or another we all have the symptoms. I've rarely been thought of as a shy person, but I remember being called to the blackboard on my second day in a high school algebra class. Step up, the teacher said. My mind went blank. Failing after three weeks in the course, I had an opportunity to switch to another class after I was elected to the school's House of Representatives. I got A's after that; the new teacher allowed me to sit quietly at the back of the room.

Another time, as an adult, I was in the studio audience of an inane TV show and froze when my name was called. Friends had set it up. The jovial emcee bounced my way with microphone in hand. My mind fogged, and I couldn't even say my name. Try as he might, the emcee couldn't get me to talk. Finally, he turned to the woman sitting next to me and began talking to her. Friends had to help me back to the bus for the trip home because I was still so shaky.

Like others who don't consider themselves withdrawn but who experience occasional shyness, I've found that being put on the spot sometimes causes anxiety.

SHYNESS IS A PROBLEM OF SELF-ESTEEM

To overcome this anxiety, Emery teaches bashful clients to take risks. "Almost all shyness problems are really avoidance and lack of self-esteem," he says.

When shy people avoid facing problems they call themselves "chicken" or "coward." Yet "we live in parallel worlds," says Emery. "One is alive and open, the other flat. If the shy person takes a risk and moves into the more positive world, his or her self-esteem goes up. If he or she chooses the flat, negative world, self-esteem goes down."

THE SECOND FORCE

Other forces are at work to convince shy people that backing down is easier and less threatening. Emery calls it the "second force."

"Sometimes we run into a second force," he says, "when, for example, a shy person tries to make friends. The more he or she desires the relationship, the more second force he or she creates. The person gets scared and makes excuses for not pursuing the friendship.

Then he or she becomes overwhelmed with the idea of trying to make friends in the first place."

To overcome some of these overwhelming feelings, a withdrawn person can create his or her own space. For example, a shy person approaching a group of people tends to remain on the edge of the group, to stand with his or her weight on one foot in a submissive posture. "That person needs to feel that both feet are on the ground. He or she should walk up to the group and stand firmly, in effect asking them to make room for him or her. Eventually they will," says Emery.

He likens the situation to a bashful child approaching a group of youngsters at play. He or she might be ignored at first, but eventually will be asked to join the group. The same is true for teens or young adults: If they go to the same gathering place repeatedly, pretty soon they will become part of the regular group there. It just happens, says Emery.

"Shyness is really fear. If people decide they don't like being shy, they can do something about it. They can learn to take note of their thoughts and feelings, and make changes."

CHANGING THE PATTERNS

These changes begin with self-induced thought patterns such as "I MUST make them like me," says New York psychologist Albert Ellis, president of the Institute for Rational Emotive Therapy. Ellis calls such thinking, "MUSTurbation."

"People come to me saying they've had a problem with shyness all their lives," says Ellis. "They put themselves down because of it, but won't force themselves to overcome it. So it's a double-whammy: They continually denigrate themselves, both for being shy and for doing nothing about it."

Shy people go through four stages:

1. They have an opportunity to approach people.
2. They say to themselves, "I must make them like me."
3. The need to make people like them is stronger than the need to interact with others.
4. Their final thought is "If I'm rejected, I must be no good," rather than "It's not good to be rejected."

It's similar to arguing with someone about a perceived offense and telling the person he or she is rotten instead of making it clear the *behavior* was rotten. Rather than focusing on the offense, the offended zeros in on the offender. Shy people go a step further by focusing on themselves and their shortcomings instead of on the situation. Shy people assume others are going to judge them harshly.

"All emotional problems are caused by what you tell yourself," says Ellis. "So I tell shy people to give up the 'must.' As long as they hang on to that, the desire to relate to another person is obscured. When you take a desire and make it a demand, you're in trouble. Shyness involves a need to do well rather than to overcome the shyness."

Many bashful people blame their inadequacies on their upbringing, says Ellis. Cognitive or emotive therapy, however, places little stock in blaming childhood experiences for the problem.

"People don't get this from early childhood. They create it by musts, shoulds and other demands. They have to take responsibility for it as adults; do something positive about it rather than perpetuate it. So they have to act differently and force themselves to overcome their shyness. They usually find that hard to do because they are reluctant to give up patterns developed over the years."

People need to change their thinking patterns to get rid of dysfunctional beliefs. "I teach them how to use the scientific method," says Ellis. "They have to rip up the false hypothesis, just as if they believed the earth was flat."

When people say they don't approach others because they are afraid of rejection, Ellis teaches them that being rejected isn't all that bad.

"Shy people are better off knowing they don't *have* to make a friend of that person. The truth is, no one likes being rejected, but no one will ever be accepted unless he or she is willing to take the risk of rejection. I tell clients to go out and be rejected five times this week so they can see they won't die from it. I tell them I'll give them a lovely funeral if they do die."

DEALING WITH A SHY PERSON

Ellis advises that if you have friends who are shy, encourage them to go out and be either rejected or accepted. "Let them know that being rejected doesn't make them bad people."

Above all, try not to reject shy people yourself, especially if you tend to be the outgoing type. And if you're dealing with a person you know is shy, slide into the friendship. Don't come on too strong.

7 MAINTAINING FRIENDSHIPS

...when you retire, relocate, divorce, or otherwise change venue

We're hurt, sometimes angry, when we lose a friend. Many things can cause the loss: death, relocation, betrayal, job change, divorce, a new marriage—or friends growing in different directions.

A DIFFERENT PERSPECTIVE AS WE AGE

A few people reported betrayal, but mostly they couldn't recall bad experiences. This may be because they had acquired a different perspective of the events through the years. Many of us mellow as we age, becoming more forgiving and understanding. We reflect on mistakes we may have made in earlier relationships and try not to repeat them.

When we open ourselves up to friendship, we also open the door to potential hurt. Along the way most of us have lost friends for one reason or another, so we know the warmth of friendship can also entail the responsibility of standing by a friend in physical, emotional or financial distress, as well as the pain of losing a friend to death.

Yet we might consider the words of Pat Wolff, community relations officer for the Department of Public Social Services in San Bernardino County, California. When her children once came home from school upset because a friend had let them down, she told them, "It's true if you don't go near the fire, you won't get burned. But you won't get warm either."

89

One woman recalled complaining to her boss that a friend with less seniority was promoted over her. She lost the friend as a result. If she had it to do over, she wouldn't go to the boss, she said.

Another reported that when she was in college her best friend stole her boyfriend, but ended up pregnant. Although it was painful at the time, 30 years later she says, "I laugh about it now."

One man said he hit a friend who was striking his wife, and after that he was no longer interested in the friendship.

"Several years ago I lost a friend to liver cancer, and I'm about to lose another to lung cancer. I can't think of any worse experience than watching a friend get sicker and sicker and being unable to do anything about it. But you *can* be there for the friend," says Phyllis Talasco of Las Vegas, Nevada.

Other ways we lose friends are more subtle than these, and we don't realize until later what we have lost.

AFTER MARRIAGE

Friendships between singles often fall by the wayside when individuals get married. Some people (especially women, according to the experts), however, realize the importance of friendships and don't allow a new life to disrupt them.

"It seems the people who are really my soulmates became my friends when I was single," says psychologist Sally Mattson. "There is something about making friends when you're on your own that's more significant than when you're a couple. When you're in a couple relationship, friendships are sometimes diffused."

Yet Mattson says wise women know the importance of maintaining existing friendships after they marry. "If you've been around the block, you know how important friendships are. Those I made before I married are my lifeline."

Although men say some of the friends they had before marriage are still their buddies, nearly all of the married men interviewed said their wives were their best friends.

Lawrence Frey, associate professor of communications at Loyola University, Chicago, explains that although married men have male buddies, when it comes to intimate sharing they turn to their wives for support and caring. On the other hand, married women typically say other women are their best friends.

Yet men and women both need intimate same-sex friendships. Unfortunately, all too often single friends are dropped by married couples, who are soon surrounded by other couples.

There are exceptions. For example, Barbara Cunningham maintains a 25-year friendship with Beverly and Dave Passon, a longtime married couple whose interest in music and art she shares. Their friendship saw her through divorce, remarriage and a second divorce. "Most married couples don't invite divorcees anywhere, but Dave and Bev like me as a person, not just as half a couple," says Cunningham.

Friends not only drift apart when one gets married; when a single person develops a romantic relationship, he or she often neglects other friendships. Several women said it angers them when a female friend's love relationship ends and she tries to renew the friendship as if nothing had happened to interrupt it. One woman says she has a friend who has had an on-again, off-again relationship with one man for years. When the couple are apart the woman is there knocking on the door. Back with the man, she is once again unavailable to her woman friend.

The woman who is called upon when her friend's romance is at low tide also has a life of her own and dates regularly. Yet she continues outside friendships despite romantic involvement.

CONFLICTS

One way of handling the conflict with the woman who drops her female friends when she is romantically involved is to confront her with the problem. Let her know how much the friendship is valued, but that it causes bad feelings when the friendship is set aside each time the romance rekindles.

People who see intimate friendships as a substantial commitment are going to have conflict, according to Mattson. "Intimacy breeds it. Those who consider friendship no more than a sort of catchall or a cultural outlet don't have conflicts because they just walk away from it. A lot depends on how important your friends are to you. Some women view spending time with a woman friend as no more than a means to an end. They go places with their friends hoping to meet men. The friendship isn't valued; it's a surrogate date until a real date shows up," says Mattson. "So much of it has to do with the individual's level of intimacy. People who don't see friendship as important to their lives don't consider solving conflicts with their friends important. I have three or four close friends and I would go to the ends of the earth to settle disagreements with them.

"The only way to understand conflict in these relationships is to recognize it," she asserts. "Minor conflicts emerge quicker than major ones. They come up in little ways, such as when someone asks, 'what do you want to do?' If you work out the small problems, the large ones are easier to work out."

To resolve conflicts, Mattson recommends:

1. Be clear about what the difficulty really is. There's a possibility that if it's trivial something bigger has been brewing; that the real problem isn't what's on the table.
2. Explain what you are upset about without laying blame; calmly discuss what you are feeling.

3. Realize that the response you get will tell you whether your friend is prepared to proceed with a conflict resolution. Is the other person able to go on talking about it without calling a halt to the friendship? If so, you have room to grow into a deeper friendship. If not, at least you tried.
4. Remember that the problem doesn't have to be completely solved in one discussion, and that the resolution might be that you have different opinions about something, but the friendship can go on.
5. Remember too that when you're talking about the conflict, the discussion can become heated and you may part on bad terms. Give it a few days' rest, then go back to it.

"Resolving a conflict with a friend is different from resolving one with a spouse," says Mattson, "usually because there is nothing, such as children, to *force* you to resolve it. It's easier to just walk away. We have to bear in mind that it's worth the trouble to learn to resolve conflicts with all sorts of people.

"My grandmother used to say that we feel so much better when we don't hold things in because there's a lot more room outside of us than inside," Mattson continues. "Working it through is best because then we don't have to carry it around. Settling a conflict is a test of friendship. We're *going* to have ups and downs with close friends; nobody feels the same every day."

Mattson believes Americans are becoming more attuned to the importance of friendship, and that by its very nature it involves conflict because we realize what is at stake.

FORGIVENESS

We pardon in the degree that we love.
—Françoise La Rochefoucauld, 17th century French writer

Those who place a high priority on friendship know that forgiveness is attendant to it. But most people need to *learn* how to forgive, says Richard P. Fitzgibbons, M.D., a Pennsylvania psychiatrist. "It is the only way to truly resolve anger and conflict."

Fitzgibbons defines forgiveness as "the surrender of one's desire for revenge."

Americans have been steeped in the tradition that it's healthy to let out anger. New research, however, shows that letting out anger does harm the one who is angry more than the one to whom it is directed. Carol Tavris, Ph.D., wrote in *Anger, the Misunderstood Emotion* that the popular belief that suppressed anger wreaks havoc on the body has been blown out of proportion. "It does not, in any way, make us depressed, produce ulcers or hypertension, set us off on food binges, or give us heart attacks."

Recent studies, in fact, show that reducing levels of anger and hostility might lower blood pressure, help us keep from becoming depressed and reduce trips to the refrigerator.

Curbing anger doesn't mean not fighting injustice or standing up for your rights. Essentially what Fitzgibbons means is that people let go of misplaced anger by doing one of three things:

1. Denying it, which is what most of us do as children and teenagers.
2. Expressing it honestly.
3. Expressing it in a passive-aggressive or sneaky way.

"There is a place for anger, but it doesn't free a person," he says. "And there is a time to keep and use the anger, as in the case of injustice. But there is too much anger in our country. We simply have to let go of some of it. Not only does it ruin friendships, but it can aggravate psychosomatic illness. Forgiveness helps reconcile relationships."

Forgiveness usually begins as an intellectual exercise and a letting go of the desire for revenge. It can then deepen to an understanding of the person who has caused the hurt.

Too often we believe forgiveness occurs quickly. It doesn't, according to Fitzgibbons. Also, some people want to keep their anger because they use it as an unconscious defense against disappointment in a relationship. The anger also protects them against becoming vulnerable.

Fitzgibbons says that as people learn to forgive they may become aware of with whom they are really angry—often themselves.

As we learn how to forgive, we also learn how to express anger appropriately, enjoy relief from emotional pain, acquire more energy (because past anger has drained us), and develop greater freedom to establish more loving relationships.

"I have a theory that people can't learn to express healthy anger until they learn to forgive. Only then does the pool of unconscious anger diminish and allow them to deal with it in an appropriate manner," says Fitzgibbons.

GUILT

Sometimes we ourselves are the cause of hostility, and we feel guilty about that.

Guilt, rather than being the bugaboo that cripples peoples'

psyches, actually makes people better citizens and more caring individuals, according to psychiatrist Marshall Lewis, M.D., medical director of Rancho Park Hospital in El Cajon, California.

Guilt has been likened to toxic waste by some therapists, but Lewis says they're wrong and are only feeding people therapeutic pablum.

"Therapists have pandered to the public's wish for quick fixes by saying, 'You're forgiven,' rather than saying, 'Well, let's look at what you feel guilty about and see if it's something you *should* feel guilty about.'"

"I think the wish to avoid pain and have pleasure (Freud called it the pleasure principle) is so universal that many therapists have found a bonanza providing temporary relief of pain by telling people they needn't feel guilty."

Guilt is a perfectly normal reaction and necessary to any caring individual. Taking appropriate action when we feel guilty about something helps us avoid hurting people in the same way again. If we feel no guilt, we will continue to hurt others.

There are time when we can't avoid inflicting hurt, but there is nothing wrong with saying to the injured party, "I'm sorry. I didn't mean to hurt you."

Basically, we simply feel better if we acknowledge our guilt, make appropriate apologies—and try never to do it again.

"People hurt themselves by not feeling guilty about things. I think people who play it straight, who follow the rules, may complain and groan about it, but in the long run they feel better about themselves," says Lewis.

"I'm saying there are situations where people should feel guilty, where guilt can be very healthy."

People don't need to drag themselves in the dirt for years and years to try to make amends, "but they do need to face whatever they have done and try to learn from the experience."

RELOCATING

When I moved from the area where I'd spent most of my adult life I was alone, distraught because of my father's death, and unaccustomed to the harsh, isolating winters of my new community. Friends called and wrote to sustain me, and one said, "This isn't how it's supposed to be. We've been reading these novels for years where people travel hundreds, maybe thousands of miles to be with a friend who is in trouble. But that is not the reality. We have families, jobs, and financial problems that prevent us from doing that."

Still, her phone call and her words were all I needed.

Recently I received word that a friend, Betty Wold, who had moved to Oklahoma, was in the hospital recovering from emergency surgery. When I called Betty in the Tulsa hospital I asked if she had help waiting when she was released. "Oh, yes! One neighbor is going to bring me dinner and do the dishes, and another is going to bring me lunch. No problem. I have so many wonderful friends," was her response.

We may not be close by to help in emergencies, but we can maintain friendships, despite great distances, by phone or letter.

My Aunt Lucille, who recently died at age 89, said of a childhood friend who is now 90, "We have had so many years. We studied together in high school, went to different colleges, taught together, thought alike, shared our experiences when we married, and are still best friends after all these decades." My aunt said a best friend is someone who loves you in spite of your shortcomings and who sticks by you always. "We still correspond often, although there are 3,000 miles separating us."

LETTERWRITING

It is by the benefit of letters that absent friends are, in a manner, brought together.
—Lucius Annaeus Seneca, 1st century Roman statesman

In our mobile society, chances are nearly all of us have friends living hundreds or thousands of miles away.

Letterwriting is spoken of despairingly by many people, and I'll have to admit I'm always behind in my correspondence. But I consider staying in touch with friends so important, and I like getting letters so much, that the effort is worth the reward—lovely letters or postcards waiting in my mailbox.

You needn't be a polished author to send notes to your friends. The best advice I ever got about letterwriting was from a college creative-writing professor. Her thoughts on the subject evolved during World War II when she corresponded with several servicemen. "You needn't write your whole life history; just hit on a couple of recent high points."

Some of the things that make for a good letter are rules used by professional writers: (1) Avoid overlong sentences. (2) Vary the length of sentences. (3) Vary the length of paragraphs. (4) Don't underline every word you think is important.

Author and grammarian E. B. White is reported to have apologized to a friend one time for writing a 17-page letter, saying he was sorry, but he didn't have time to write a shorter one.

A short, newsy letter brings warmth into the recipient's life. It's a gentle nudge that says, "Hey, I care, and I'm thinking about you."

Phyllis Talasco corresponds with a woman in another state with whom she became friends during the years when their children were growing up. " We were Brownie and Girl Scout leaders together, she was my son's Cub Scout leader, and both our boys played Little League baseball. We had lots of great times together, and some not so great, and we have remained friends all these years. I think of her now and then, and if people are not out of mind when out of sight, they can remain friends forever!''

MOVING UP

People who don't recognize the importance of friendships often dump friends as they move up the career ladder.

"Sometimes we want to change our image, and we let go of friends because they are an embarrassment to us," says psychotherapist Shirley Harrison. "Perhaps one has been a blue-collar worker and moves up to a white-collar job. He or she doesn't have the strength to say, 'These are good friends, and if my new friends don't like them, too bad. They are still my friends. Like Liz Taylor marrying a general contractor: She's saying, 'This man is okay, and if you can't accept him, it's your loss.' ''

People who value friendship look askance at dropping friends because of a change in status. Yet the same change can cause the person left behind to end the friendship. He or she, unwittingly feeling jealous or inadequate, may write off the friendship with the excuse that the other person has become snobbish.

If the friendship is valued, the person who feels hurt should confront the other and settle the subtle conflict before it robs both parties of a treasured relationship.

RETIREMENT

Dorothy S., a 64-year-old real estate agent, dreads the word retirement. "What would I do with all the spare time on my hands?" she asks. "My business keeps me in contact with active people."

Workers have divergent views of retirement. It isn't the given it was a generation ago—work until your mid-60s, receive a gold watch, then move to a retirement community.

The retirement-age population is the fastest growing segment of our society and will account for one-fifth of the U.S. population by 2020. Mature people are healthier and longer lived than ever before, and the government is promoting later retirement in the face of projected Social Security difficulties by establishing a schedule of increased benefits for those who defer retirement. A constantly rising cost of living also gives older workers an incentive to stay on the job.

A more important incentive, however, may be needed social contact. Many people retire only to find they are bored and feel useless. Retirement takes not only careful financial planning, but a realistic view of how it will affect a person's social life.

Not everyone can take a late retirement, of course. The older you get the more likely you are to have health problems, says Kingsley Davis, a senior research fellow at the Hoover Institution, Stanford University. Further, he says, "The dreamlike retirement existence envisioned in the United States and other industrial countries, with time to fish all day or golf every afternoon, is dubious.

"Human beings fare poorly under conditions of perpetual recreation," he continues. "Job loss often takes away not only money but friends, status and purpose. There is a tendency to withdraw and become isolated, so it's wise to make friends off the job."

In today's world, elderly people can't count on their children being nearby since their work often involves moving far away. So retirement presents a dilemma. "Some people are happy with the work they're doing and needn't retire. Others aren't so happy and can't wait to leave,'' says Davis. ''People have a hard time defining what they really want.''

If people do decide to retire, presuming they have a choice, they need to consciously work at a support system. ''Stay active,'' Davis advises. ''Get out and meet people. Remember that other people are also looking for friends.''

DEATH

''I don't do funerals,'' an acquaintance once said to me after I told him about reading a tribute at a friend's funeral. My friend's daughter had written it but was too grief-stricken to speak the words herself.

''What do you mean?'' I asked him.

''I don't attend funerals. They're too depressing,'' he said, adding, ''Some people seem to like them, though.''

''Excuse me!'' was my retort. ''People don't attend funerals because they like them. We do it to support the family and friends who are left behind. Anyone who *likes* funerals probably is a sicko.''

I proceeded to give him an example. I had recently attended the funeral of a longtime writing companion whom I hadn't seen in years. The funeral was held in the city she had lived in most of her life, although she had spent her last years in a retirement community some distance away. When her daughter thanked several of us for attending, she said, ''I didn't know mother had so many friends who would remember her. She was a wonderful person and it makes me feel good to see you all here.''

By the time most of us reach age 50, we've experienced some losses and understand grief a little better than we did at 20 or 30. Letting go is something we must accept. We may not like it, but that is of little consequence.

We all suffer losses, more of them as we age. They not only create voids in our lives, they reaffirm our own mortality.

A 63-year-old man recalls, "My best friend was my best man at my wedding. We talked and shared mutual problems from grammar school through college. He died about 20 years ago in a small-plane accident, but I think of him often."

A 75-year-old woman says of a best friend, "We became neighbors in Fresno in 1954, and we were close from then on, wherever we were. We just meshed. She died in 1978."

A 59-year-old writer reflects: "She was a fellow writer. We used to sit and read each other's work over coffee in the kitchen, forgetting the rest of the world. We were very much alike and admired each other—as writers, as women, as mothers. She died of a brain tumor, but I consider myself lucky to have had a friend like her in my lifetime."

An 81-year-old man says he still has several friends from childhood: "But they are dying off."

Lasting friendships are always subject to change, and the most painful change, of course, is death.

8 OBSTACLES TO FRIENDSHIP

. . . *mind drift, loaning money and other annoyances*

All potential obstacles presented in this chapter can be overcome. We can become more comfortable about money-lending decisions, improve conversational skills, learn to enjoy the moment, evaluate our emotions when we allow others to impose on us, and help ourselves become the friend we want others to be.

FRIENDS IN TIME OF DISTRESS

When interviewing people for *Survivors of Suicide*, a book for family and friends left behind when someone takes his or her own life, I found that friends offering the bereaved love and support helped most. They didn't have to really *do* anything but listen and be there for the grieving person.

The same is true of family and friends of those dying from AIDS. Because there is an undeserved stigma attached to AIDS, support is critical to its victims and their families and friends.

Yet some people carry a need to help others too far; an alcoholic's co-dependent, for example. Sometimes the motive isn't love, but a dysfunctional need to act as a caregiver.

Many provide care to children, and to aging parents, but those roles come to us in the natural order of events. And caring individuals want to help friends who are sick or having problems. That's what

103

friends are for. But when illness or some other trouble is a friendship's sole cohesive force, we need to reevaluate what's happening and try to strive for a healthier relationship either by walking away from that one, or by confronting the other person.

Making an uncomfortable decision like confronting someone or ending a friendship forces us to deal with such thoughts as becoming cynical or unfeeling. Sometimes we need to be reassured by friends or a therapist that wanting to help others is natural and healthy, even if we make mistakes once in a while.

FACTITIOUS DISORDER

Mark Feldman, M.D., attending psychiatrist at Hill Crest Hospital in Birmingham, Alabama, reports the case of a woman who told a support group she was in that she had cancer. She enjoyed being the center of attention, and continually reminded others of her illness. Later, she told the same group that her grandfather had been seriously injured in a fire. Eventually her stories made the other members suspicious. They discovered she had been lying to get attention, and they confronted her.

Feldman calls the condition "factitious disorder": a need to invent symptoms in order to be treated like a sick person and get attention. In its extreme form it's also called Munchhausen syndrome, named for a character in German fiction who told elaborate battlefield tales. Feldman says people with either condition have a need for nurturing, sympathy and companionship, and most get away with it because friends and family don't want to confront them with their suspicions.

The psychiatrist says the woman who faked cancer eventually moved to another state after friends and acquaintances abandoned her, which isn't unusual. Those suffering from the condition often start over again with similar stories in their new location.

"There is a pragmatic issue, other than draining people," Feldman explains. "I spoke with a law student in California who had put her education on hold while she helped a boyfriend who allegedly had cancer. He later fled the country, and it turned out there was nothing physically wrong with him." The woman was upset because not only had she lost money, but her education had been interrupted. To get her back on track, Feldman recommended therapy.

"It's difficult for the layperson to understand factitious disorder. People wonder how the caregiver could have been so foolish. But people who offer help have nothing for which to apologize."

Once we recognize what has happened, Feldman says, "We may have to be sensitive to the fact that we may be misled sometimes. We may encounter milder forms of factitious disorder, and it is up to each of us to decide when it has gone far enough. We all tolerate things like this and we have to set our limits. There are lots of risks in confronting a person. When you do, you can unleash anger or depression. We have to decide if it is important enough to risk whatever the result of the confrontation may be. In some cases, the friend feels so violated he or she has to walk away from the relationship."

Feldman's story illustrates an extreme example of people sometimes termed "psychic vampires." They drain you emotionally, sometimes financially, and keep you from attaining your own goals.

PSYCHIC VAMPIRES

I was contacted by a woman in the town where I live shortly after my book *When Your Parents Need You* was released. She told a sad tale of being forced to care for her tyrannical aging father. She had no freedom, the doctors were on his side and told her what to do, she'd had to give up her home and move in with him, and her own health was failing. I told her about support services, caregivers who can come into the home, and other available forms of relief.

She would hear none of it. After listening to her unrelenting self-pity for about an hour, I asked whether she would inherit a substantial amount from her father if she cared for him as he wished. When she acknowledged that she would, I told her she had a choice: to get out on her own and make something of her life, or continue living under oppressive conditions in order to inherit the money.

It was clear by the time I left, choosing never to meet with her again, that she preferred to continue suffering.

It's not uncommon to find people who continually complain about tragedies in their lives. They use others as sounding boards and drain them. We never feel good after being with them, and if we continue to see them we need to ask why we allow ourselves to be pulled into situations that make us feel so bad. Does another person's despair make us feel superior or more worthwhile?

Tabloid newspaper publishers know the public likes to read about the tragedies and alleged faults of others—especially notables who seem to have everything going for them. We can say to ourselves, "Well, I might not be beautiful (or handsome), have lots of money, or be well known, but at least . . .

If we use these same rationalizations in choosing friends, we might be the ones needing emotional help.

SUPER POOPER SCOOPERS

Gail Kawanami Allen of Life Works Consulting Services in Santa Ana, California, calls people who like to take on others' problems "Super

Pooper Scoopers." Their egos are fed when they can pity others. Often when the person with the trouble conquers it, the pooper scooper feels slighted, even angry at the individual who no longer needs his or her close attention and help.

"Usually, he or she will go find someone else who's willing to confide his or her problems," says Kawanami.

TRAPS FOR THE ELDERLY

The elderly are particularly vulnerable when it comes to listening to others' tragedies, according to clinical psychologist Laurence Grimm. "It's sometimes difficult for the elderly to make friends, and often those friends are sick or have other problems that can come with aging," he says. "As we get to know someone, we share our lives, and when older people become more isolated they have less to share. One reason some of them talk about symptoms all the time is that they have nothing else to talk about. I would caution elderly people to look for other commonalities."

MONEY MONSTERS

He that wants money, means and contents is without three good friends.
   —William Shakespeare, English dramatist and poet

A more famous line of Shakespeare's is "Neither a borrower, nor a lender be; for loan oft loses both itself and friend, and borrowing dulls the edge of husbandry."

Several people acknowledged losing friendships over money—

and not only because of borrowing. We have profound hang-ups about both the lack and the abundance of money. Americans seem able to talk openly about nearly anything except finances. Many marriage and family counselors say that money problems break up more marriages than sexual ones. We even hide the amount of money we lose in gambling casinos and how much we actually spend on lotto tickets.

Families have been estranged, friendships terminated, over money. And borrowing and lending take their toll.

Barbara Booth, counselor and director of the Women's Center at Rio Hondo College in Whittier, California, says, "I know from personal experience how that can ruin friendships. I never loan *or* borrow money. I think a lot of people feel obligated to give a friend money when he or she asks for it. They don't know how to get out of it. They haven't learned to say no. A loan can ruin a friendship even if it's repaid, especially if the lender felt he or she couldn't say no; the lender feels taken advantage of. If someone asks to borrow money from me I'll suggest we brainstorm to find a better way to take care of the person's problem. Often there *is* another solution."

A week after I met a woman who seemed to share similar views and whose work touched bases with my own, she asked to borrow money. I turned her down because my first instinct was that she was taking advantage of me. It seemed inappropriate for her to ask so soon after we met.

Ironically, many of those interviewed who said they loaned money to a friend said it was the other person who broke off the friendship when the debt wasn't repaid.

One said, "I had to ask for the money back and that broke up the friendship." Several said they didn't consider money important enough to end a friendship over.

Other comments:

- "I loaned a small amount to a friend and never saw or heard from the person again."
- "Loaning money can kill friendships and families."
- "I always loan money unconditionally, without expectations."
- "I don't consider money enough of a problem to lose a friend over."
- "I've loaned money and lost a friend over it. But I think it was more my attitude than my friend's that caused a change in the relationship."
- "I had to ask for a loan to be repaid and it ruined the relationship."
- "I've never been asked, but I don't think I would do it."
- "Some friends I loaned money to paid me back and it solidified the friendship. Some didn't pay me back and I resented it."
- "I've loaned money and it made bad feelings between us."
- "I have loaned money. Sadly."

Consider the following rules for loaning money:

1. Never loan more than you can afford to lose.
2. Consider whether the potential borrower is reliable.
3. Don't ask what the money will be used for: Your values are different from your friend's.
4. If you're asked for a large loan, suggest a bank; perhaps you could co-sign.
5. If you grant the loan, do so with no expectations.
6. Don't feel guilty if you decide to say no.

SPECIAL PROBLEMS

Some years ago I became acquainted with a minister's wife who was taking a class at a local junior college. She confided that it was difficult for her to make close friends with people in her husband's congregation because of jealousies. She would have liked to become better acquainted with several of the women, but it just wasn't possible; all in the congregation expected like treatment.

Ellen Livingston, a Unitarian minister, says her husband, Nick, loves to entertain. "He likes to invite compatible people to small parties. But we can't do that within the congregation—we can't form what would seem like a clique."

CHANGE HAS ITS BENEFITS

Although Livingston faces the same problem clergymen and their wives have traditionally had to deal with, she spoke positively about changes she's seen within the clergy since women (although still few in number) have entered the profession.

"It used to be that when we met for conferences, the male ministers would sort of practice oneupmanship instead of sharing friendships. They would brag about how many speaking engagements they'd had, how many new members, etc. The women coming in have been a catalyst for change: We talk about sermons, sharing, our commonality. It's a much more loving atmosphere."

CHATTER MATTERS

When we're getting acquainted, our conversational styles may determine whether or not a first meeting develops into a deeper friendship. First impressions *do* last.

Some people clearly have the knack of making others feel they are special, even in a brief meeting with someone they have just met. And there's more to being a great conversationalist than being witty. "You've got to put your heart into it," says James Lynch, Ph.D., coordinator of the University of Maryland's Center for the Study of Human Psychophysiology.

Great conversationalists are genuinely attentive to other people and what they have to say. They're good at picking up cues that tell them what others are interested in. They are curious, and if they don't know much about a subject, they ask questions then listen to the answers—which boosts the other person's self-esteem.

Asking questions makes them participants in conversations rather than passive listeners, and they gain reputations as interesting conversationalists who always seem to attract people at gatherings.

They don't try to impress others with their expertise on a wide range of subjects; they do focus on the person they're talking with and what he or she is saying as though that person and that conversation were the most important thing in their lives at the moment.

To hone conversation skills, experts recommend:

- Deciding ahead of time to be interested in the other person.
- Not agreeing with everything the other person says.
- Not praising too much; that can be construed as insincere and/or patronizing.
- Listening for cues to what is interesting or important to the other person.

- Responding to information by acknowledging it and asking questions.
- Occasionally asking the other person to repeat what he or she has just said.
- Forgoing demanding words like "should," "ought," "must" and "have to."
- Forgoing absolute words like "always," "never," "nobody," "everybody" and "every time."
- Avoiding apologetic prefaces such as, "I'm sorry, but . . ." when you disagree.
- Curbing the habit of repeating such phrases as "you know" and "do you follow?"
- Using the words "we" and "our" more than "I" and "my."
- Letting the other person know you don't know it all and really want his or her opinion and/or advice.
- Occasionally asking for clarification of a point made by the other person.
- Not trying to impress others with your knowledge.
- Starting off with simple subjects rather than trying to shape world events.
- Using anecdotes when explaining something; telling funny tales about yourself can be very appealing.
- Speaking clearly and directly.
- Maintaining eye contact without trying to stare down the other person.

BODY AND HAND MOVEMENTS

Body movements that destroy conversation include rubbing your nose, pulling your ear, shifting weight from one foot to another, rocking, pacing, jingling pocket change, twirling a strand of hair, stroking a mustache, cracking your knuckles, and even smiling too much. When we're uncomfortable, we sometimes smile to ease tension— but a smile at an inappropriate time can be distracting.

In *A Psychology of Gesture* Charlotte Wolff, Ph.D., says that "the whole body can participate in the language of gesture, whilst verbal language is restricted to the organs of speech."

Hand movements reflect how we view the world, our work, our friends and acquaintances, and ourselves. In turn, we can tell much about how others view us or the situation by their hand movements.

Movements such as nail-biting can reveal something about an individual's inner state. We assume that nail-biters are nervous or worried, but the habit can also signal insecurity, as can placing one thumb over the other or carrying the hands in one's pockets.

Hand movements are more powerful than most people suspect, and politicians, clergymen and actors have learned how to use them well.

Some telling hand gestures:

- If the fingers are generally spread when hands are in a relaxed position, it usually means open-mindedness and openness toward others. If hands are clenched and fingers cramped *even* in a relaxed position, it usually means narrow-mindedness.
- Relaxed hands are usually slightly curled, but the greater the curl, the less secure the person feels.
- Palms together, hands in coat pockets with thumbs out, or hands on coat lapels indicates confidence.
- When the little finger stands out on its own, away from the other slightly curled fingers, it generally means the person tends to be individualistic.
- When only the ring and little fingers are curled toward the

palm, the person is afraid to speak out. The topic of discussion might be a sensitive one, or the person may not yet have all the facts.
- If the ring finger is the only one curled and the rest are straight, the person is deliberately withholding information.
- A clenched fist can be either good or bad. A gently clenched fist shows positive determination; a tightly clenched fist may show unrealistic determination, anger or frustration.
- A tightly clenched fist with the thumb tucked beneath the fingers indicates a miser, not only in financial matters but in the approach to life.
- When the thumb is tucked into a loose fist, the person may feel guilty, be trying to hide some past event, or be anxious about something.
- When the thumb is stiff or looks as if it is tied down to the hand, the person feels intimidated.
- Hands clasped with fingers entwined indicates the person is contemplating a next move; conversely, when the hands are together and the fingers *aren't* entwined but the thumbs are wrapped around each other, the person is waiting for your next move.
- Rubbing the palms together can mean cunning.
- Placing the hand on the face or nose, or stroking the chin, indicates the person is evaluating the other person.
- Pointing an index finger, holding hands tightly clenched, wringing the hands, making fistlike gestures or running a hand through the hair is a sign of frustration.
- A hand placed on the breast signifies an understanding attitude.
- Crossing the arms or rubbing the eyes means the person is suspicious of you or what you are saying.

- Hands placed behind the back indicate an attempt to size up a situation. The person may feel temporarily unsure.
- When a hand is placed on a table with the fingertips and heel of the hand touching the table, the higher the arch between them, the greater the person's uncertainty.

Hand movements and positions can tell us a lot about people—including ourselves.

MIND DRIFT

Most of us suffer occasionally from mind drift, or an inability to stay tuned to the here and now. I've always had great admiration for people who can clear their heads, focus on the matter at hand, and refuse to let other issues interfere. I recall a consultant in a Girl Scout bowling league who, beset by other troop leaders with questions and problems, would respond with, "Not now. My mind is on bowling."

When she taught knot-tying, that's where her mind was. Nowhere else. She was therefore a great teacher. And when she spoke with you, you were the center of her attention.

When we're talking with friends we often start thinking about the argument we had with a child that morning, or the frozen chops we forgot to put out to thaw for dinner. Before long our minds are adrift with all sorts of problems; we catch only bits and pieces of the conversation, add nothing of our own. This mind drift robs us of one of life's biggest pleasures: enjoying the moment, tuning in to the here and now.

Tuning out turns others off, and it can cause accidents. How many times have you nearly if not actually bumped into another car or run a stop sign because your thoughts were elsewhere?

Drifting from a conversation may not seem as threatening as crashing into another car, but the outcome can be serious. It can be a lifelong habit that cheats us out of full participation in life, says Irwin Jay Knops, professor of psychology at Emory University in Atlanta, Georgia.

"Politicians are good at giving you that 'moment,' that handshake, even though they aren't registering it at the time. They train themselves to give the impression they are focusing on you. If politicians can learn to do this, so can the rest of us. We can give others our complete attention, and make ourselves popular. Some people have this skill; they focus and are truly remembering you," he says.

Knops, who specializes in treating children with short attention spans, says people who want to break the mind-drift habit must convince themselves that it's important to stay focused, and that it requires a change in attitude.

Too many people believe that what they have to contribute to society is unimportant.

"A person doesn't have to be a passive influence in the world," says Lewis Picher, a Denver, Colorado, clinical psychologist who works with depressed patients. "A person's attitude can pull him or her out of a seemingly boring situation. It can be difficult to do, but you can train yourself."

Picher recalls one client who was still depressed over a two-year-old divorce. She tried to socialize with others, but while she was with them her mind continually drifted to her ex-husband and the bitterness she felt. She was living a passive life.

Few people seek help for what they believe is a minor problem. "Who cares if I drift out of a conversation?" many think.

But the problem is worth attention, especially if one has a problem making friends. In our fast-paced society, with its emphasis on communication, it's important to stay in tune.

Knops offers a suggestion to bring you back to the here and now if your mind starts to drift: Simply bite your lip hard enough to jolt you back into the picture.

Picher suggests another technique: "Shout loudly in your mind, 'STOP!'" The word jolts consciousness.

It's important to make people we deal with feel special, even though at times it is difficult to keep a high attention level. Some people seem to believe it's up to others to keep them from being bored—but it's clearly a matter of changing their own attitudes.

HEARING LOSS

Another problem that interferes with friendship, especially as we age, is hearing loss. In fact, more than two-thirds of older adults in the United States have some degree of hearing impairment.

The condition needn't mean a traditional hearing aid is needed, however. New technologies and techniques such as telephone amplifiers and therapy to enhance listening strategies offer hope to the hard of hearing.

Unitarian minister Ellen Livingston says several people who attend her church are clearly trying to make friends, and are just as clearly hampered because they either are unaware that they suffer hearing loss or are too stubborn to do anything about it.

Yet it is one of the fastest growing disabilities in the country, according to Julian Kopit of Self Help for the Hard of Hearing (SHHH), a national organization with chapters in 48 states and 17 countries.

Hearing loss affects people in one of two major ways:

"People with 'conductive' hearing loss, in which sound doesn't reach the inner ear for physiological reasons, hear themselves clearly, but can't hear others," says Wiley Harrison, M.D., hearing specialist and adviser to the American Hearing Research Foundation. Conductive hearing loss can be caused by excess ear wax, fluids, abnormal bone growth, infection, noise pollution—and the aging process itself.

A second problem is "sensorineural" hearing loss. It also involves inner ear problems, but forces the person to speak louder in order to hear him- or herself. With this type hearing loss, sound passes through the outer and middle ear but becomes distorted by a defect in the inner ear.

"Central" deafness is a third but rarer type of hearing loss caused by damage to the brain's nerve centers. Central deafness makes it difficult to understand language rather than creating problems with sound levels. Certain medications, fevers, head injuries, extreme exposure to loud noises, circulatory problems and tumors are a few major causes.

In general, when we begin losing our hearing it's due to speech ranges, not sound. "Consonants are at the higher end of the range, vowels at the lower end. Most people who have hearing loss have problems with higher ranges, so spoken words are missed because consonant sounds are shorter and harder to detect even without hearing impairment," says Kopit.

Distance from the source of a sound also makes a difference, of course.

Acoustics, too, account for the way we hear sounds as they bounce from walls, plants, automobiles, etc. Add interference from other noises in the room or on the street, and hearing can become a problem for anyone.

These "outside" or "interference" noises are what keep manufacturers working on better hearing aids. The problem is that it's difficult to curtail surrounding noises and make a tiny amplifier that picks up the voice sounds we want to hear.

Because a majority of the hard-of-hearing have a low tolerance for loud sounds, some hearing aids limit the volume that is let in.

Another help is a T switch that allows the wearer to disconnect a hearing aid microphone and connect it to a telephone receiver.

"What's red-hot right now is digital hearing aids," says Kopit, adding that so far, advertisements for such devices are more impressive than the product. Kopit cautions that as yet no consumer rating system exists for hearing aids. It's wise, therefore, to try several different types before purchasing one. SHHH headquarters in Bethesda, Maryland, gives demonstrations at no cost and will provide lists of places throughout the country that offer similar demonstrations.

Spillover from the Americans With Disabilities Act, which goes into effect beginning in 1992, will also help the hearing impaired. It requires upgraded facilities and accommodations, and anti-discriminatory practices, to benefit the handicapped. According to Alison Sutton, also of SHHH, among other things the law will force airline terminals to install TV monitors so the hearing impaired can view messages concerning take-offs and landing, and buses must be equipped with amplification devices so the driver can be heard when he or she calls out stops.

Other accommodations for the hard of hearing include assisted listening devices such as amplified headphones in movie theaters, meeting rooms with enhanced listening systems, and amplification devices in public sites such as jury rooms. "Many elderly are disqualified from jury duty because of hearing problems. Under the new law, they will be allowed to serve," says Sutton.

Bell Telephone Co. recently installed more than 55,000 pay phones equipped with amplification devices. Also, telephone companies dealing with the general public must offer systems such as TDD, a device that allows communication by phone through a typed and printed relay system. GTE offers the device free on loan to those with severe impairment. Hard-of-hearing people should check with their telephone companies to find out if they qualify.

Tom Frank, Ph.D., professor of audiology at Pennsylvania State

University, cautions that not all listening devices are the same, however, and urges consumers to shop around for the ones that suit them best.

Frank and other hearing specialists teach patients listening strategies, both on and off the phone. Standing close to a person when talking with him or her and watching both mouth and body movements can give a hearing-impaired person clues about what another person is saying. They also encourage anticipating what the other person is going to say, either on the phone or face to face.

Another strategy is to repeat instructions given over the phone; for example, "Yes, I'll meet you at seven at the theater." If the message has been incorrectly received it can then be corrected.

Besides improving hearing through advanced technology, scientists are working on ways to correct the loss itself. Research at the University of Washington, thus far involving only animals, indicates that new cells can be grown in the ear to replace cells damaged by exposure to loud noises.

A hearing checkup may be called for if you have any of the following symptoms:

- People complain that you're not listening to them.
- You confuse words you hear and sometimes get the wrong message.
- You frequently ask people to repeat what they have just said.
- You understand men's voices better than women's. (Women's higher-pitched voices are more difficult to hear.)
- Other people's voices sometimes sound like static.
- It's difficult for you to hear such things as a ticking watch, crickets, or running water.
- You argue with others that the television isn't loud enough.
- People frequently ask you not to speak so loudly *or* so softly; either can signal hearing impairment.
- There is a history of hearing loss in your family.

The following agencies provide free or minimal-cost services and information concerning hearing problems:

American Academy of Otolaryngologists Inc. (professional organization of physicians specializing in diseases of the ear), 1101 Vermont Ave NW, Washington, DC 20005.

American Hearing Research Foundation, 55 E Washington St, Chicago, IL 60602.

American Speech-Language-Hearing Association, 10801 Rockville Pike, Dept AP, Rockville, MD 20852.

Captioned Films for the Deaf (supplies catalog on request), 5000 Park St N, St. Petersburg, FL 33709.

Occupational Hearing Services in Media, Pennsylvania (call between 9 A.M. and 6 P.M. Eastern time for a number to call in your area that will give an over-the-phone hearing test); 800–222–EARS (222–3277).

Self Help for Hard of Hearing People Inc. (SHHH), 7800 Wisconsin Ave, Bethesda, MD 20814.

9 CELEBRATE YOUR FRIENDSHIPS

. . . laugh, dance, enjoy and reminisce

CELEBRATIONS AND RITUALS

The morning sun forced its way onto the orange-colored Arizona mesa, bathing it with warm-toned streamers.

On a smaller scale, it warmed our bodies and toasted my 14-year-old son's cheeks, causing him to squint at the surrounding terrain. He made a slow 180-degree turn, soaking up the energy around him, and said, "I understand now why Native Americans worshipped the sun."

Whatever makes people celebrate—the radiant sun, a birthday, a promotion, the autumnal equinox, the publication of a new book, rain after a drought—is sure to be followed by peace within. We were designed to celebrate. Devoid of rituals, lacking joyous outbursts, humdrumming our way through work and sleep and food we would shrivel into obscurity.

And large or small, celebrations take on more meaning when they are shared with a friend.

"Celebrations and rituals, no matter how insignificant they appear, are heavy with meaning. They provide roots and foster a deeper sense of purpose and significance in our lives," says Carlfred Broderick, University of Southern California sociologist and psychologist.

We need no special holiday in order to celebrate. The book *AIDS, a Self-Care Manual* recommends that if a friend is dying of AIDS,

"Celebrate holidays and life with your friend by decorating the home or hospital room. Bring flowers or other special treasures. Include your friend in your holiday festivities. A holiday doesn't have to be marked on a calendar; you can make every day an occasion."

Many people with life-threatening illnesses learn to live each day in celebration. John-Roger and Peter McWilliams write in *You Can't Afford the Luxury of a Negative Thought* about strengthening the process of living by setting a goal not to live for a certain number of years, but to live life fully in each moment. "If you take good care of the moment, the years will take care of themselves," they say.

We can celebrate birth, death and all the life in between. We can set our own agendas and include friends in our personal celebrations. Not because it's on the calendar, but because it's in our hearts.

Special holidays, of course, are laced with meaning. Days like Halloween and April Fool's Day, say mental health experts, allow us to break the rules of a restricted and technological society. Days like Thanksgiving and Fourth of July touch base with our past and our future; they add stability to our lives.

Celebrations have been used to bring diversified peoples together; for example, Mardi Gras breaks down the barriers between the wealthy and the needy. In the explosive France of the 16th century, Catherine de Médicis recognized how much celebrations tempered hostilities. She funded huge festivals to bring people together who under different circumstances would have been killing each other.

When Marie Antoinette said, "Let them eat cake"—if she truly did—she may have been recognizing the importance of celebration in stressful times rather than showing insensitivity toward the starving.

We starve ourselves when we limit celebrations with our families and friends. They provide nourishment in the present, dessert when we reminisce about them later.

MEMORIES

The memory is a treasurer to whom we must give funds, if we would draw the assistance we need.
—Nicholas Rowe, 17th century English dramatist and poet

We've heard the phrase, "All he or she has to live on are memories." Well, he or she is lucky. Health professionals now know that reminiscing is not only good for the soul, it boosts our health. Most happy remembrances involve time shared with others.

Early studies by Fred B. Bryant, psychology professor at Loyola University, Chicago, showed the most well-adjusted college students reminisced about fond childhood memories. Furthermore, the happiest elderly people routinely drew upon happy memories.

More recent studies by Bryant show a link between depression and lack of joyous memories. "There is good evidence that older people who don't reminisce are among the most depressed," he says. "There is a definite link between depression and the absence of happy memories."

TYPE A'S AND TYPE B'S DIFFER IN MEMORIES

Studies also show differences between hard-driving type A personalities and the more easy-going type B's. While type A's seem full of vitality, drive and happiness with their work when they're younger, they are among the most depressed as they age. "They are directed toward the future and don't reflect on good times. They seldom keep scrapbooks or celebrate with friends unless it's to recognize an achievement. They therefore have smaller support groups because they want to control everything and are unwilling to reach out to others," says Bryant.

"This serves them well while they're younger because their values are being fulfilled. Then sometime in middle age their worlds shift. They can no longer do 50 things at one time, and they feel they are losing control."

So at a time when they need support systems and happy memories to keep them going, they are adrift with neither. Conversely, the type B personalities have crept along at a slower pace but have taken the time to establish support systems and store fond memories. And they thrive.

"Type B's are happier and better adjusted in middle age and beyond," says Bryant. "They have a richer base from which to draw. They not only have shared their own joys with others, but they have also celebrated their friends' joyous moments. Past middle age, type A's start reporting less happiness, while the happiness factor of B's goes up."

NEGATIVE MEMORIES CAN BECOME POSITIVE

People who call up pleasing reminiscences smile more often to themselves, according to Bryant. In fact, if we're enjoying happy memories and negative ones interject themselves, we can choose to push the latter from our minds. "Most people have unpleasant memories, and that's okay. If we shut off all memory in order to avoid the negative, we're also shutting out the positive. If we just let our minds take over, then shut out the negative memories when they come, the positive will take over. Positive thinking is a skill that can be developed," he says.

FROM NEGATIVE TO POSITIVE

My sister, Theda, and I had just come from a court hearing at which we were appointed conservators for our mother. The drive home from Los Angeles gave me time to mull over the day, which began in gloom and showed no signs of improving. Then we went to Philippe's, a New York-type deli near downtown. During lunch Theda and I talked about growing up in the 1940s on Ninth Avenue off Jefferson Boulevard in Los Angeles.

So we sat on stools in Philippe's grousing about how poor we'd been until the man next to me interrupted, saying he'd grown up in the same area. The conversation turned to the fun times in the old neighborhood: the old-fashioned candy store, the vacant lots with weeds that tasted like licorice, trips to the old Clifton's Cafeteria downtown, Bard's theater with its double matinees loaded with cartoons, rides on the streetcar.

By the time we left the deli, my sister and I were in a different mood. Reminiscing had triggered happy memories of people and places. Life was not the gloom of the morning's court hearing; it was transformed by a series of happy memories.

HAPPINESS IS MORE THAN NOT BEING DEPRESSED

In the process of developing a positive outlook on life, it is important to recognize that the mere absence of depression doesn't mean you're happy. "Just because you're not down, it doesn't mean you're up," says Bryant. "Coping strategies for happiness are separate skills. Friends help us enjoy happy times. They add joy to our memories."

The primary strategy for developing a positive outlook on life is friendship, says Bryant. "Friends should be more than help in bad times; they should share good times."

RECALLING MEMORIES

To get the memory bank rolling, Bryant recommends sitting in a comfortable place, closing the eyes and trying to re-create past happy times. "Imagery is more effective than looking at photographs, which is a passive way to remember. When we use photos, we only recall what we see. With imagery, we're part of the action."

To store a wealth of positive memories Bryant also recommends:

- Learning to enjoy the moment and capturing joy to store it for later.
- Planning ahead and looking forward to celebrations, gatherings with friends and going places.
- Reflecting on those happy times.

For those who lack reminiscing skills and would like to tweak their memories, Bryant recommends the book *The Life Review* by Robert Butler. Butler defines life review as a universally occurring mental process in which people recall life experiences, evaluate them, and attempt to reconcile values adopted over their lives with what their lives have actually been.

MEMORIES THROUGH THE SENSE OF SMELL

Sometimes without our even trying to conjure up memories, they come to us in a whiff because they are also available through our sense of smell.

We smell without the awareness we have of other sensory perceptions, so sometimes a memory tumbles into place and we don't know where it came from. But a moment's reflection and parts of our lives come flooding into our minds like bubbling sulfur springs.

"We now know that the same part of the brain that allows us to experience odors is responsible for controlling emotions, sex and memory. It's the limbic system, which is the oldest part of the brain," says Milton Wolpin, professor of psychology at the University of Southern California.

Our primal ancestors used their acute sense of smell for survival, and ancient Romans and Greeks drew on various vapors to influence people's behavior. While some Eastern cultures remained more in touch with the healing and mood-altering effects of aromatic plants and herbs, Western culture turned instead to chemistry and synthesized drugs. Today, however, we're reevaluating the sense of smell.

Research indicates:

- Natural body orders produced by male and female hormones play a role in attraction and mating.
- Infants have an acute sense of smell that helps them bond to their mothers.
- Certain fragrances can induce muscle-relaxation, enhance creativity, alleviate stress, reduce pain, increase productivity, vitalize athletic performance, set the stage for specific dreams, and trigger long-forgotten memories.

SMELL MEMORIES

I was hiking with a friend when he picked up an orange-colored leaf that was not yet brittle, crumpled it between his fingers and placed it to his nose. "Once we smell something, it's never forgotten. It's always somewhere, rumbling around in our minds, and when we smell it again, it triggers a memory. But most people don't pay that much attention to smell," he said.

I have long remembered his words. I remember him, too, when I'm in the forest.

We smell. We feel, taste, see and hear, believing we've experienced it all.

The smell of rain triggers memories of small children for me.

One night thunder and lightning brought one child tiptoeing to my bed. Another cried and I lifted her from her crib and placed her with us beneath the covers. Drapes and window wide open, we watched the lightning, heard the thunder, and breathed sighs of relief when the rain finally touched down. I told them how Hera and Zeus, Greek mythology's queen and king of the gods, argued or made love, bringing on the thunder's clash.

A combination of fresh rain, my son's sweet leathery smell and the creamy aroma of my daughter's curls remain. It is a wonderful memory.

A salty, seaweedy smell brings visions of sand dunes and feckless romping on the beach when I was young.

The mountain canyon where I lived smelled of smoky pine, oak, apple wood and eucalyptus on chilly mornings when I went out walking. I reflect on those walks fondly.

And I recall Zoltan, an old hermit who lived in those mountains, through a memory of smells. Once when I visited him I grabbed the skillet in which he was frying hamburger and threw it out the back door.

"Wha'd you do that for?"

"It's spoiled. Rotten. Stinks."

"Didn't bother me," he said, admitting to no sense of smell at all. Too many broken noses. Too many fights. He told me about those fights, and laughed. They were actually pleasant memories, and I shared them with him.

Heady stuff for a simple whiff, but oh what magnificent memories an inhaled flutter of air brings!

MEMORIES WITH MUSIC

Music helps us recall different life stages. We hear a marching band and we perhaps remember a colorful parade we've watched. Perhaps it takes us back to a time we stood on the sidewalk, sun beating down on our shoulders, friends gathered around in celebration.

We hear a ballad and maybe we picture ourselves sliding across a dance floor; perhaps it makes us get up and dance to an unheard melody from long ago. The memory warms our souls.

Occupational therapists S. L. Bennett and F. Maas wrote in the *British Journal of Occupational Therapy* about how a music-based life review assisted by health-care professionals can help improve an elderly individual's personal adjustment. "As the history of music parallels the history of human beings, it can serve as a springboard for discussion of past and present concerns," they said.

MUSIC ASSOCIATION

"One aspect of music that makes it unique for each individual is the associations a person makes with a particular piece of music," said Alicia Ann Clair, Ph.D., music therapist at Colmery O'Neil Veterans Affairs Medical Center in Kansas. "The association may be direct or indirect. That is, the music may have been heard only in one context or situation and whenever it's heard it is a reminder of that particular moment in time. Or a piece of music may have a certain style that is generally associated with a time period in one's life. These associations may be very happy, or they may be very sad—even remorseful. They are so individual that they are impossible to predict, and a song that evokes smiles and happiness in one person may trigger tears and grief in another."

Clair's statements about music were given at hearings for the U.S.

Senate Special Committee on Aging's study of how music affects the elderly. Theodore Bikel, musician, actor and president of the Associated Actors and Artists of America, also testifying at the hearings, said, "Human beings are in need of music—indeed of all the arts—not as a frill or a luxury, but as a basic necessity. Many senior citizens may lose strength and vitality but they do hold on to the memories of their youth. Anything that evokes these memories puts them in a brighter and happier frame of mind."

WE'RE ALL MUSICAL

Frank R. Wilson, M.D., associate clinical professor of neurology at the University of California, San Francisco, says, "All humans are innately musical; by this I mean we are biologically endowed with the ability to create and respond to music. This aptitude is as deeply rooted in the nervous system and as integral to life as is the gift of language."

Our musical memories touch the very fiber of our being; they connect us to friends of old, and to time spent with friends now and in the future.

FOODS CAN TRIGGER MEMORIES

We tend to forget how closely social functions and food are entwined.

Whenever I eat blackberry jam I remember picking berries by the bucket on the hills near my grandmother's farm when I visited one summer. That particular memory leads to others about my summer on the farm.

One friend gets nostalgic about the hot cocoa and cinnamon toast his mother used to make when he came home cold and tired from trick-or-treating on Halloween.

Another friend remembers how the pineapple tasted on a trip to Hawaii.

Our memories of food are so great that one hot summer day I wrote about popsicles for a newspaper column I used to do. I gathered the information from the staff and from calling the popsicle company.

Does the column's text trigger any memories for you?

Diets be hanged. Forget about red dye number whatever. Pay no attention to red or blue tongues. Don't think about sugar content. Forget suave manners, haute cuisine and feeding your cells with nothing but vitamins.

It's time for popsicles.

Maybe it happens once a year—when the weather starts getting hot and muggy, and you remember the carefree days of childhood summers past and want to be anyplace except cooped up in an office or dusting the furniture.

About the only thing that satisfies at such a time is a popsicle.

I remember . . .

. . . blue popsicles, double-sticked, that fell apart when you were halfway through and then split down the middle and started sliding down the stick, only to run down your hand.

. . . whacking the popsicle—just right—on the counter as you paid and the popsicle broke in two so it was never messy. But you had to whack it just right.

. . . saving 1,000 or so wrappers to get a 15-cent prize.

. . . my brother making Christmas decorations out of the popsicle sticks.

. . . making a popsicle key holder that looked like a miniature fence.

. . . how about the log cabins we used to make?

. . . oh yes, I used to get them at Hines Hardware Store in Chesire, Connecticut. Used the sticks during the summer for crafts and during school as a counting device.

. . . I used to make boats and float them down the gutter.

. . . I still like popsicles when I'm sick.

. . . We could break them in two and share with a friend.

The column went on to give the history of popsicles, including the fact that in the 1930s the twin popsicle was invented, so that for a nickle two friends could share the treat.

It is great to have friends when one is young, but indeed it is still greater when one is getting old. When we are young, friends are, like everything else, a matter of course. In the old days we know what it means to have them.

—Edvard Grieg, 19th century Norwegian composer

10 NOTABLES SHARE THEIR VIEWS OF BEST FRIENDS

Ed Asner, actor, defines friends as people who "take time out from their cares to care for you."

Lew Ayres, actor, who became a peace activist after starring in the movie version of *All Quiet on the Western Front*, says, "A friend is someone who, like God, has undying faith that we will change our ways and prevail even though the whole world may know our weaknesses and infamy."

El Bradley, television news commentator, says a friend is someone "who cares."

Anita Baker Bridgeforth, singer, says a friend is someone who "knows you quite well, but loves you just the same."

Dame Barbara Cartland, author, says, "A real friend is someone you can trust not only with your life but with your husband."

Phyllis Diller, comedian, says a friend "listens and is loyal."

Jack LaLanne, physical-fitness expert, says, "Friends are people who will sacrifice anything they own to keep you—no questions asked."

Ed McMahon, television personality, says a friend is someone ''who asks you what you want before you even request it.''

Cesar Romero, actor, says a friend is someone who ''understands your weaknesses and puts up with you through good times and bad.''

Dennis Weaver, actor, says a friend is someone who thinks of your needs as though they were his or her own.

BIBLIOGRAPHY

Melvin Kinder, *Going Nowhere Fast*, Prentice Hall, 1991.

Deborah Tannen, Ph.D., *You Just Don't Understand*, Ballantine, 1990.

M. Scott Peck, M.D., *The Different Drum*, Simon & Schuster, 1987.

Ashleigh Brilliant, *I Feel Much Better, Now that I've Given Up Hope*, Woodbridge Press, 1984.

Victor E. Frankl, *Man's Search for Meaning*, Simon & Schuster, 1984.

Carol Tavris, *Anger, the Misunderstood Emotion*, Simon & Schuster, 1982.

Joanna L. Stratton, *Pioneer Women: Voices from the Kansas Frontier*, A Touchstone Book, Simon & Schuster, 1981.

Samuel P. Oliner and Pearl M. Oliner, *The Altruistic Personality: Rescuers of Jews in Nazi Europe*, Macmillan, 19—.

Robert Ornstein and David Sobel, M.D., *The Healing Brain*, Simon & Schuster, 19—.

Introducing our new series of Newcastle originals: 'the Living Well Collection'. This creative line of books will provide solid, comprehensive information and advice for people over 50 on lifestyle, finances, relationships, health and fitness, careers, housing, retirement, and much, much more.

50 & STARTING OVER **$10.95**
Career Strategies For Success

YOUR PERSONAL FITNESS SURVEY **$12.95**
A Guide To Your Current State of Health

BLUEPRINT FOR SUCCESS **$12.95**
The Complete Guide to Starting a Business After 50

LIVING WELL **$12.95**
Answers to Life's Practical Mysteries

Spring 1992 **THE FRIENDSHIP BOOK** **$12.95**

Spring 1992 **LONGER LIFE, MORE JOY** **$12.95**

Spring 1992 **WHEN YOUR PARENTS NEED YOU** **$9.95**

If you are unable to find any Newcastle book at your local bookstore, please write to:
    Newcastle Publishing Co., Inc.
    13419 Saticoy Street
    North Hollywood, CA 91605

INDIVIDUALS: To order any of the books listed in our catalog, please fill out order form, check the number of copies of each title desired, and enclose check or money order for the full amount plus $3.00 postage and handling for the first book ordered $1.00 for each additional book. Calif. residents please add current sales tax with each order.

    NEWCASTLE PUBLISHING CO., INC.
    P.O. Box 7589, Van Nuys, CA 91409, (213) 873-3191, FAX (818) 780-2007

VISA AND MASTER CARDS ACCEPTED   **$15 MINIMUM ORDER**

Free, complete, current catalogues are available upon request. Just send us your name and address and we will send you a catalogue.

Quantity discounts are available to groups, organizations and companies for any Newcastle title. Telephone (213) 873-3191 or FAX your order to Newcastle Publishing Co., Inc. at (818) 780-2007.

Thank you for your interest in Newcastle

ORDERS:
1-800-932-4809

AL SAUNDERS, Publisher